Like Sheep

by Donna L. Smith

illustrated by Gary J. Smith

Dedication:
To our parents and grandparents,
whose wisdom and world view
informed our own...

Leroy Images LLC
P. O. Box 247
Washington Island, WI 54246
email: info@Like-Sheep.com

Acknowledgements:
with appreciation to:
Dr. Susan Rock, for assistance in proof reading
Courtney Cauldwell, for production assistance and marketing

Table of Contents

Who could have imagined that a childhood dream
could become a real life adult adventure?

Preface

When I was a little girl in rural Pennsylvania, our farmer neighbors, the Harveys, bought a flock of Hampshire sheep to add to their assortment of Holstein dairy cows, pigs, ducks, chickens and guinea hens. Hampshire sheep have white wool, but their legs and faces are black, as if they were wearing masks and black stockings. They are sturdy and handsome.

Mr. Harvey had been working hard all that spring, clearing a twenty acre parcel of scrub brush and trees, to make a new pasture for the sheep. He wasn't quite ready when the sheep arrived in early summer, so his middle daughter, Deemay, was given the job of tending the sheep until her father could get the pasture fenced in.

Each morning Deemay led the sheep out into the field, stayed with them all day, and brought them back into the barnyard in the evening. There they were safe from the wild dogs which roamed around our countryside in those days. These dogs could do a lot of damage to unprotected livestock, and sometimes did.

Deemay was a real shepherd, the first one I ever knew. She was about fifteen years old at the time. Though it seems remarkable to me now, she occasionally allowed me to spend the day with her. My mother packed my lunch in a little metal sand box bucket and sent me walking up the road toward Harveys' farm.

Together Deemay and I led the flock out into a grassy open area. There we sat down on the ground and, basically, watched the sheep eat all day. They always tended to stay together, but if the flock moved too far one direction or the other, Deemay and I just walked around them and nudged them to come back.

At noon, as we ate our lunches, the sheep lay down for their afternoon rest. It was fun to watch them all chewing their cuds at the identical same rate of speed. How could all these sheep chew in unison; up, down, up, down, all together?

Toward evening, when the sun started to set behind Penrose Hill to the west, Deemay and I moved the sheep down toward the creek, over the plank bridge, up the lane and across the gravel road into Harveys' barnyard. Another day of tending sheep was over.

I was only five at the time, but Deemay wasn't babysitting me. She actually seemed happy to have my company. Maybe conversation with a talkative little girl was more entertaining for her than were she to be alone with just the sheep all day. In any case, I fell in love with sheep that summer. I knew that someday I wanted to be a shepherd too.

Being a shepherd was a dream I kept in the back of my mind as I was growing up, going to high school, and then to college. Later I taught school and raised a family. I did a lot of other interesting things too, but I never gave up the idea that someday I would have a flock of sheep.

When I was in my early forties, I finally got my chance. That was when my husband and I moved to his family farm in Wisconsin, to look after his elderly father. While my husband commuted to the city to continue his work, I settled onto his family's 19th century farmstead.

My father-in-law was very pleased when I planted a vegetable garden, and a strawberry and raspberry patch. I mowed our large lawn and tended the many flower beds that he could no longer care for. Best of all, ...I kept a promise to myself! I got a small flock of large, white, and very gentle Columbia ewes. There were just thirteen of them at first.

I bought the sheep from Mr. McCoy, a farmer who was reducing the size of his flock. These were all senior citizen sheep, with the exception of one spirited ewe lamb, who had jumped on the truck with the others. Mr. McCoy told me that the ewes were all expecting lambs in the spring. Thus my grand shepherding adventure began. I could hardly believe that after thirty five years of waiting, my childhood dream was actually coming true!

For the next thirteen years it was I who was a shepherd. At one point my flock grew quite large in number, but usually I kept only about forty ewes and their lambs, and one or two rams.

It did not take long for me to realize that being a shepherd is very hard work. My flock was utterly dependent on my doing a good job. If I were lazy or uninformed, my sheep suffered. If I were diligent and caring, they thrived. If I made good decisions, they were safe. If I made bad decisions, they were not. Sometimes things went wrong even if I had done everything right.

Fortunately, my family's farming background had prepared me to accept hard work, but I soon learned that there is a lot more to caring for sheep than just hard work. This book tells about some of those other things; the remarkable, the sad, the funny. It recounts some of the lessons I learned from my experiences. All the stories are true, even though at times the truth may seem to be stranger than made up stories could possibly be.

Chapter 1: <u>Sacrifice Lamb</u>

My sheep arrived at our farm early one November morning. I was very eager to get to know them, but, unfortunately, they were terrified of me. I could not even get near to them.

When I fed them in the barn, they ran as far away from me as they could. They huddled so tightly together that I was afraid they would trample one another. These sheep obviously knew that I was not their real shepherd, and even though I wanted to care for them, they did not trust me even a little bit.

I could see that I would have to be quite patient if I wanted things to change, so I moved very slowly whenever I came to feed them. I spoke very quietly when I was around them. I spent a lot of time in the barn, just sitting and talking to them. I was trying to let them get accustomed to being with me.

Gradually, as we moved through that first winter, the ewes began to settle down. We were not exactly friends yet, but over time, as I proved myself faithful in caring for them, they began to relax and to trust me a little bit. I began to feel encouraged.

One snowy morning in late January, as I stepped into the barn to do the morning feeding, I was greeted by the smallest, most plaintive little voice I had ever heard. I followed the sound until I spied a new baby lamb, no bigger than a stuffed toy. What a surprise!

She stood beside her mother in the barn aisle. She was still a little wobbly on her feet, but she was already dry and fluffy. She obviously had been born sometime in the middle of the night. The wool in her little coat was tightly curled and she was all white, except for a remarkable black patch around one eye.

Her mother looked down at her and seemed to me to be very proud. Occasionally mama reached over to lick her little daughter's back and tail. This is how mother sheep encourage their lambs to nurse, but I didn't know that then.

Oh, I was so excited. My first lamb! She had been born about six weeks earlier than I had expected, but that didn't matter. She was beautiful, and I was thrilled to meet her. I picked her up. She seemed to weigh almost nothing. "Six or seven pounds," I was thinking. "About the size of a newborn human baby."

Now it was time to show how much I had learned from my sheep raising books. Holding the lamb in front of me, leaning partly over, I backed away from her mother. In this awkward manner, I "led" the mother ewe into a special small birthing pen, designed to give her and her new baby protection and privacy. I certainly did not want this little darling to be hurt by a stray step from one of the other ewes.

I gently laid the new baby on the straw in the corner of the pen. Her mother ran to her side and began bleating softly, as the lamb answered. I retreated from the pen and closed the gate behind me.

After I had brought fresh water and hay to the mother, I ran quickly to the house to call my friends. I wanted to tell them the good news.

On the way to the phone I thought of naming the lamb, "Switch!" The black patch around her eye reminded me of an old magazine ad where a fellow with a black eye is saying, "I'd rather fight than switch!" He meant he was sticking with his brand of product, no matter what anybody said.

So "Switch" she was, because of that black eye, and what a little character she turned out to be. I never knew before that a lamb could be so clever or so cute.

Over the next month this little ewe lamb brightened up each day with her antics. I found her sometimes running a mad dash, up and down the aisles of our old barn. Sometimes I'd find her asleep, actually lying on top of her sleeping mother's thick coat.

Switch and I became fast friends. Since I was the ONLY shepherd she had ever known, she trusted me. I was astonished at how quickly she grew. Her little legs and back rounded out until she was almost chubby. I loved her so dearly and could hardly wait until mid-March, when the other lambs were due to be born. What anticipation! What fun!

Can you imagine, then, my sickening panic and dismay when, one morning in late February, I looked all over the barn for Switch and finally found her in obvious agony, her legs stiff and quivering. Before I could get to her, she fell down. When she tried to get up, she staggered, then fell over again.

She weighed about twenty pounds by this time. She had appeared to be so healthy and strong the night before. What possibly could be the matter with her now?

I raced for the phone to call the veterinarian in town. At first the vet was a bit puzzled too. Finally he suggested, "Maybe she has 'White Muscle Disease'. Have you given her an injection of selenium?"

"Selenium?" My mind went racing. I knew that selenium is a mineral, and that human beings need small amounts of it in their diets. None of my sheep books had mentioned anything about selenium injections for sheep, however.

"Oh yes," said the vet. "Our soils here in Wisconsin had the selenium leached out by the big glaciers long ago. You have to give the lamb selenium or it will die from a condition where the muscles spasm and then don't function. White Muscle Disease, they call it."

Our farm is on an island which lies out in Lake Michigan. Getting to town in the middle of winter to buy selenium was not an easy prospect. I moved as quickly as I could, but by the time I was able to give Switch a selenium injection, it was too late. My little lamb princess died a couple of days later.

I tell you, I cried like a baby. I cried because I loved her and I missed her. Most of all, I cried because I realized that it was my own lack of knowledge which had cost her life.

My best intentions had not been good enough. My research had not been complete enough. My response to her need had not been quick enough. I wanted to be a really good shepherd, but clearly I had not been good enough for my little "Switch".

I hurried to visit my shepherd friend, Ingrid. I sat in her kitchen and cried as I told her what had happened to "Switch". Ingrid knew how sad I was, and was very kind to me. She tried to comfort me by saying that we could be thankful that we had learned what was wrong with Switch.

I did want to feel thankful! My beloved lamb was dead! What I felt was really hurt and sad and guilty!

I knew Ingrid was a good person, however, and I knew that her advice could be helpful. Reluctantly, I listened to her, and tried to begin to think of things I could be thankful for.

I knew that I was thankful for the joy this little lamb had given me. I knew I was also thankful for all of the sheep, and for how much I loved tending to them. I was thankful for the kind vet who had tried to help me with my lamb, and then, suddenly, it struck me hard!

"Ingrid!" I heard myself shrieking. "If Switch had not been born early, and if we had not learned about selenium because of her, we might soon be looking at a couple dozen or more dying lambs!"

Oh my goodness! The same mistake of not giving a selenium injection to each lamb after birth would have resulted in the certain death of ALL of the lambs to be born that spring, both Ingrid's and mine. Switch, by coming early and by dying had, in fact, saved all the other lambs who were yet to be born.

Didn't I already have their selenium injections purchased and waiting for them? Switch had been a "Sacrifice Lamb". Her death was a sad loss, but it was also a great salvation for all the other lambs.

Now I really did start to cry. I could see now how much worse it could have been. "Switch" would have died anyway, and so would have all the other lambs, had she not been born early.

Sure enough, within a couple of weeks, the other lambs did begin to arrive. I faithfully gave each one of them a small injection of selenium a few days after it was born. There were no other lambs with "White Muscle" disease that year. All the lambs were healthy. They all grew up to be fine adults. In all the seasons that followed after, I never again had another lamb with White Muscle disease.

Many years have now passed since these events took place. As I tell you the story about the most fortunate loss of my beautiful ewe lamb, "Switch", I am surprised to find myself crying again.

Chapter 2: <u>Lessons In Tending Sheep</u>

Right from the beginning I decided that I would keep written records on every sheep in my flock. Mr. McCoy, the farmer from whom I bought my old ewes, had placed a numbered tag in each ewe's right ear. As I named each ewe, I recorded her name and number in a record book.

The names I chose were rather fanciful; names such as Aurora, because she was very lively, Carrot, because she especially liked them, Mensa, because she was very smart, Miss Piggy, because she actually looked like the puppet character, and Big Mumma, because, well, because she was a very big mumma.

Over the years I wrote down important things that happened in the lives of the sheep. I enjoyed reading from my record book, my little sheep biographies. I started writing on the first day the sheep arrived.

After Switch died, there were sixteen additional lambs born that first year. During the birthing season, I was kept busy running back and forth from the house to the barn, helping with things the ewes needed for their lambs. It was good that they were experienced mothers and had no trouble knowing what to do. It was all so exciting that I danced with happiness.

I had hoped for lots of little ewe lambs. That way I could build my flock quickly. When lambing was over, however, there were twelve little ram lambs and only four little ewes.

"That's O.K.," I told myself. I named each lamb, and marked his or her name in my record book. Then I noted how much each had weighed at birth, the date, and any details I knew about the birthing.

I tried to choose names for the lambs which made sense. For example, "Lazarus" was the name I gave a little ram who had needed "mouth to mouth resuscitation" when he was born not breathing. I figured that since he had come back from the dead, he needed to be given the same name as the man in the Bible who had also come back from the dead.

I named one set of twins, a ram and a ewe, Jack and Jill. A set of twin rams was born on March 15th, the "Ides of March". That is the day in history when the Roman Emperor, Julius Caesar, was deposed by his enemies. I named those lambs, Julius and Ides.

My favorite lamb was a large, handsome ram, with beautiful kinky wool and a strong, gentle spirit. He weighed twelve pounds at birth. His twin brother weighed only six pounds.

"Hmm......", I mused. "What does this remind me of? "

"Why, Jacob and Esau, twins in the Bible story," I thought. Sure enough, one lamb was strong and hairy, while the other was small and not so elegant, just like the Bible characters. I named the lambs, Jacob and Esau.

I weighed each lamb every week in order to see how it was growing. I was amazed to learn that the lambs averaged a three to four pound weight gain every week. By the time a lamb was a month old, it weighed around twenty pounds.

While I had really enjoyed watching Switch bounce and run all over the barn yard, now I had a virtual lamb Olympics going on. All sixteen lambs raced around together, and leapt and circled up and over their resting mothers. They acted like children on a playground. There were leaders and followers, shy ones and bold, bigger and smaller ones. I never, never tired of watching them.

My friend, Ingrid, said one day, "People must think we're crazy when we say, 'I think I'll go have a look at the sheep', and then we don't come back into the house for an hour or more." Ingrid was just like me; entranced by watching.

I loved my sheep. It was as if I had my own little village filled with characters, as in a movie or a book. Other people looked at my sheep and saw a bunch of white wooly bodies. I saw a real community, made up of individuals, each with his or her own distinct personality, likes and dislikes, and history. I could recognize each sheep, even at a distance, and could call him or her by name. I felt as if we knew each other.

Though the sheep couldn't speak English, that didn't mean they couldn't communicate with me. I began to notice, for example, that sheep have "body language". A drooping head is not a good sign, because it means that sheep feels sick. Stomping front feet means they are angry. Wild ranging eyes mean they are afraid.

It is true that sheep make a "Baaa Baaa" sound, but all "Baaa Baaa's" do not mean the same thing. Some are cries for help, or of alarm. Some mean, "Wait for me!" Some are saying, "Well, hurry up then!"

The sounds that are the most touching are the soft, deep rolling murmurs the ewes give to their lambs. They sound so loving and intimate that there is no mistaking the intent of that ewe to care for her young, and to defend it, even to the loss of her own life. Sheep are usually prone to turn and run from danger, but if a ewe has lambs, she will stand to fight, ramming any intruder whom she thinks has bad intentions for her baby. I learned that fact once or twice when I was toppled from my feet by an overly protective ewe.

As the spring and summer of that first season wore on, I learned new things about sheep every day. The shearer came to cut the wool off the sheep, just as he would do every year thereafter. I was amazed at how quickly he gave the sheep a hair cut. I was more amazed, when he was finished, that the wool lay all in one neat blanket on the floor, waiting to be rolled up and bagged. The shearer was a very skillful man.

After the shearer had shorn a sheep, and while that sheep was already turned over on her haunches for the shearing, I trimmed her hooves. The sheep's foot is divided into two hoof parts, like two big toes. This is unlike a horse, whose hoof is just one big round part.

Trimming sheep hooves is like cutting gigantic toenails. If the hooves grow too long, the sheep will become lame. Trimming is done with a special knife or a pair of hand held hoof clippers. It must be done very carefully, to keep from cutting the hoof too short and causing the sheep's foot to bleed.

Sometimes I accidentally made a mistake and cut the hoof too deeply. Then the sheep's foot would bleed. When that happened, I sprinkled corn starch on the sheep's foot in order to help stop the bleeding. I always felt so sad when I hurt one of the sheep, but they never, never cried out when they were in pain.

Besides trimming their feet, sheep needed other regular attention as well. Three or four times a year I gave worm medicine injections to all the sheep. I did not want any of my sheep to die from an intestinal worm infestation.

When the lambs were small, I banded their tails with a special, strong rubber band. In a few days their long tails would fall off from lack of blood circulation, and the sheep would have short tails from then on. This "docking" of tails is not for the sake of appearance. It is done to protect the sheep from what we call a "Fly Strike".

Flies like to lay eggs in any moist place in the sheep's wool. If that occurs, and if the eggs hatch, the fly larvae attack the sheep's skin and can actually break through into its flesh below. That is a very, very nasty and painful thing for a sheep. By keeping a sheep's tail short, the moisture from its normal elimination cannot be trapped so easily under its tail. Thus the awful effects of a "Fly Strike" are prevented.

Sheep, like cows and horses, are grazing animals. They eat a variety of grasses and low growing broad leaf plants. Over time I learned which plants the sheep liked, and which ones they did not.

Our pasture had been seeded with a legume called "Bird's Foot Trefoil." It is related to clover, and was named "Bird's Foot Trefoil" because its leaves looks a little like a bird's foot.

Although the trefoil in the pasture looked green and luscious to me, somehow the sheep preferred many of the weed plants which grew along the fence rows. One weed plant which they particularly liked was poison ivy.

After a couple of years they had completely eradicated all poison ivy from our farm. That was a good thing for me, but still a surprise.

Oh my! When that first summer came to an end, I was shocked to realize that I was going to have to sell most of my ram lambs. No flock can safely keep a dozen rams. There can only be one dominate ram in a flock. If I kept all those rams, there would be a lot of fighting to find out who that dominate ram was going to be. I did not want that to happen.

As fall approached, I began to visit the flock just to watch the ram lambs and to think about which one I wanted to keep. This was going to be an important decision, because the future of the flock would depend on my making a good choice. Whichever ram lamb I chose would be the father of the next season's lamb crop.

It didn't take me long to realize that I loved each one of those ram lambs, and I really didn't want to lose any of them. I decided that it had been a big mistake to name all of them, and I vowed that in the future I would not name any lamb I did not intend to keep.

After thinking and thinking, and watching and watching, I finally made up my mind. I decided that, because of our remote location, I would keep two ram lambs instead of just one. That way I would be assured of having at least one good ram.

To keep them from fighting with each other, I figured that I could divide the flock into two groups, and put one ram with each group. Now I just had to decide which two ram lambs to keep.

The first choice was easy. It had to be Esau. He had grown up to be a very handsome ram. He was gentle and good natured. His back was straight and strong. His legs and feet were even and sturdy. His wool was still just beautiful, with the desired crimp and texture. I knew his wool would make great yarn.

Deciding on a second ram to keep was not going to be so easy. There were eleven other candidates; rams who had all grown fast and were all well formed.

I can't actually remember what I was thinking about as I decided, but I ended up keeping Julius. I knew that he was handsome and strong, but I really think it came down to the fact that I especially liked his mother, Aurora. Her temperament and mothering skills were exceptionally nice, and I thought perhaps Julius' daughters would be like her. I hoped in turn that they would give me lots of strong, healthy and happy lambs in the future.

And so it was determined. I would keep Esau and Julius.

It was a very sad day indeed when the truck came to take the other ten ram lambs away to be sold. I felt so bad for their mothers. To tell the truth, I actually felt guilty. It didn't seem right that their lambs would be taken away from them, when they had cared for them so well.

If the ewes minded terribly, I couldn't tell. I may actually have felt worse than they did.

After the ram lambs were gone, the barn seemed rather empty. There were no more lamb Olympics, that wild racing up and over the manure pile in the barn yard. There were just four ewe lambs, and Esau and Julius. I think they missed their playmates.

The autumn days were getting short now. In Northern Wisconsin it often gets cold early in the autumn. After the blaze of leaf color, the rains come, and then, soon enough, the long snows. I could hardly believe that a whole year had gone by since I had bought my sheep from Mr. McCoy, but here it was again, another November.

Now that the weather had turned cold, and the grass was no longer growing in the pasture, I began hauling hay and oats, twice a day, to feed the sheep. They began to stay pretty close to the barn, where they could find shelter from the winter weather.

I looked forward to another lambing season, not too far in the future. I was happy, because winter put me and my sheep together in close quarters. They were aware that I was the person who brought the food to them each day, and they had learned to trust me quite a lot during our first year together. It seemed to me to be a wonderful family feeling of close living, and of shared experience.

Over the many years which followed, I grew to be very intimately related to this flock of sheep. It is surprising what a close relationship animals and people can develop with one another. The animals depend on their human caregiver, but, in truth, the farmer also depends on the animals for his or her own livelihood.

Julius, it turned out, was the champion ram in the end. From all those records I kept, I learned that it was his daughters and granddaughters who produced the most and the best lambs over the years.

My sheep proved to be fun loving creatures, capable of caring for each other, and even capable of caring for me at times. While my experience with sheep taught me something about genetics and animal behaviors, I also learned a number of things about myself. That was a bonus I hadn't anticipated when I began my adventure.

I learned that I was capable of providing sustained care for my flock, and was worthy of their trust. Gradually, my experience became an important part of who I am. I grew along with my flock. I cannot begin to tell how much my animal friends enriched me, and taught me to value the gift of life in new and deeper ways.

Not long ago we had a visiting pastor at our church. He announced that he planned to preach a sermon on the passage in the New Testament about Jesus' being the "Good Shepherd".

As a way of making an introduction to the subject, he asked what he thought would be a question just for illustration. He said, "Has anyone in this congregation ever actually been a shepherd?" He fully expected the answer to be "No!" and then he intended to explain to the people what he had read about sheep and about how they behave.

When he had finished asking his question, I raised my hand. I didn't speak, but in my heart I was saying, "Yes, I was a shepherd for a number of years. I already know everything you are going to tell us about sheep, and much more."

When I think about being a shepherd, every muscle in my body is filled with the memory of what it takes to be a good shepherd to one's flock. I can remember how diligent I was called upon to become, and how much energy I spent. I can recall being up through many long winter nights. I can even look down and see numerous scars on my hands, scars I received in the course of caring for my sheep.

I also think of the deep friendship I had with woolly, four legged animals. I am thankful to be one of a relatively few people in these times who know personally what the Bible illustrations mean when they talk about sheep and shepherds.

And then I have my record books. They remind me of the sheep I have loved, and of our adventures together. Reading them helps me to remember......

Chapter 3: <u>Running Around in Circles</u>

As anyone who has kept even a dog or a cat can tell you, animals make messes which need to be cleaned up. A cat can be trained to use a litter box and a dog can be what we call, "house trained", but let me assure you that sheep are not so tidy.

We call the waste from sheep and other large farm animals, "manure". Any farmer who cares about animals will do his or her best to keep barns and barnyards clean and dry. That necessarily means dealing, somehow, with manure.

I always used straw for bedding. Our barn was old, and I did not have any power equipment, so when the straw became messy, I had to set about the hard task of cleaning the barn with a shovel, scraper and wheelbarrow.

I didn't really mind doing this dirty job, but one must always be careful while doing it, because manure produces nasty gases. They can burn a person's nose and eyes, or actually make him or her sick. That is why I always waited until we had a cool, sunny day before I cleaned the barn, a day when the chemical activity of the manure was lessened.

One day, several years after I had begun caring for sheep, I was in the barn cleaning out manure. By that time I had about fifty sheep who were very accustomed to having me around. In fact, they hardly noticed me as I worked.

I must admit that I wasn't paying much attention to them either. My mind was on other things. I HAD noticed, however, that some of the sheep were resting inside the barn and that the remainder of them were lying down outside, in the barnyard.

After a while, a couple of ewes on the inside of the barn got up and stretched. Then they began to make their way slowly toward the door at the northwest corner of our old dairy parlor, the part of the barn we used for a sheep fold. Pretty soon I noticed that a couple other ewes had also gotten up and were meandering toward the door, following after the first two ewes.

This was not unusual. As you probably already know, sheep are what we call "flock" animals. Most breeds of sheep tend to stay close together in everything they do. They play "follow the leader" a lot. One old ewe is usually the "leader", and she generally decides when it is time to go out to eat, and when it is time to come in to rest. All of the other sheep tend to follow her leading and to do whatever she does.

As soon as these first four sheep got up and headed toward the door, several more sheep inside the barn, as if on some invisible signal, also got up and started to follow them. When the rest of the sheep in the barn saw them get up, they all got up too, shook themselves off and started to line up to go. It appeared it was time to move back out to the pasture. Siesta was over! "Get movin'!"

Just about that time, however, some sheep from the barnyard came in through the opposite doorway to the dairy parlor, the southeast doorway. I think they had probably intended to come into the shady barn to lie down.

Seeing, however, that the inside sheep were now on their feet and in motion, they felt inclined instead to stay standing, and to begin to wind their way through the aisles of the barn, following in the same direction. They soon joined the tail end of the parade of inside sheep slowly making their way toward the outside.

All would have proceeded normally, I suspect, had not some of the remaining outside sheep, whom I could see lying in the yard to the west of the barn, gotten the idea that maybe now they should be coming into the barn too. As they hurried to catch up with the sheep who were just entering the barn, their movement caught the attention of the very first sheep, the ones who had just now been exiting through the opposite doorway, heading toward the pasture.

But now, instead of continuing in that direction, those first sheep felt suddenly compelled to turn and follow the sheep whom they had just seen disappearing around the south end of the barn.

As I was shoveling, I had begun to notice all of this development's taking place out of the corner of my eye. About this time, however, I stopped working altogether. I stood leaning on my shovel handle, just watching. I sensed that something very unusual was about to happen.

The sheep who had first started out of the barn now caught up with the sheep who had been the last to move toward the southeast doorway on their way into the barn. As they hooked on to the tail end of that line, I realized that the entire flock was now, incredibly, linked together in one big undulating loop. They were following each other out one door, around the barn, in through the other door, through the barn and then out the first door again.

At first I started to chuckle to myself, and pretty soon I was laughing out loud. This was by far the silliest thing I had ever seen sheep do.

At the start they moved slowly, as if nothing were so unusual about their following after one another. As the parade continued to circle around and around, however, they began to go faster and faster. Wooly body followed after wooly body. There appeared to be no leader at all, just many followers going around in a gigantic circle.

"Oh my!" I wondered. "What is going to happen here?"

I sensed that the sheep themselves were also beginning to get a little worried. By now they had begun to go quite fast, and were starting to huff and puff with their effort. Though they appeared to know that something was wrong, they seemed unable to stop themselves.

Around and around and around they went, getting more and more frantic all the while. I actually began to be concerned that if some poor old ewe might stumble and fall, she could be injured by the onrushing sheep coming behind her.

21

I stood considering what sort of intervention to make, when suddenly, with a tremendous burst of energy, one old sheep, who was heading out the northwest doorway, did NOT turn left and circle around to the south again. She pushed straight forward, as if by great determination, and moved, instead, northwest toward the pasture.

She had not gone very far before she stopped and looked around. The whole flock had followed her, and were now just milling around in the barnyard with their heads down. They were all panting.

I may be wrong, but it seemed to me that the sheep were quite shaken up by what had just happened to them. They certainly looked tired.

After a little while they all composed themselves and quietly headed single file out to the pasture, yes, in a great and gentle parade. It was as if nothing unusual had occurred at all.

I stood there just observing them for some time before I returned to my own work. "What would have happened," I found myself asking, "if one sheep had not resisted her instincts just to 'follow along'? What would have happened if she had not instead decided 'TO LEAD'?"

Chapter 4: <u>The Sound of a Voice</u>

You may have heard somewhere that sheep know the sound of their own shepherd's voice, and that is true. Do you recall my telling you about when I first got my sheep? Those old ewes were terrified of me, because they had not yet come to trust me. Mine was not the familiar voice of their shepherd.

As time went on those sheep, and their sons and daughters and grandchildren, grew accustomed to me. I could call to them when they were out in the field, and they would come running to the barn if they thought I had something good for them to eat. They definitely grew to know my voice. That was rather amazing.

Perhaps the more amazing thing to me, however, was that I, after some time had passed, also began to understand their voices. It is a mystery to me how this happened, but there were many times over the years that I may have been in bed sleeping, when suddenly I sat up, wide awake, and listened to the sounds coming from the barn. Then I would get dressed, go out into the dark night and walk the hundred or so feet across the yard outside my bedroom window to the barn.

This rarely happened without my discovering exactly what I had been called out for. It was frequently a ewe in labor. That means she was in the middle of giving birth to her lambs. I assisted in many deliveries of lambs. Trouble sometimes arose when there were multiple lambs to be born or when a young ewe was having her first lamb. I marveled that I had become so aware of my sheep that I also heard their voices, even when I was fast asleep inside my house.

One day a funny, but touching, event occurred. I had gone to the grocery store and upon returning home was carrying my bags of groceries into the house from my car. I noticed a young ewe named Tiffany standing at the corner of the barnyard nearest the house. She was bawling with all her might, and I know it may seem strange to you, but it sounded to me as if she were saying, "Put those bags down and get over here this minute. I need your help right away! Hurry! Hurry!"

Well, I did just that. I couldn't imagine what her problem was, but I did not question that she wanted me to come, and to do it quickly.

When I got to her side I was puzzled. I noticed nothing wrong with her. She wasn't limping and she didn't look sick. As I approached her, she turned away from me and circled around to the south end of the barn. I followed her, and then I saw what her problem was.

While I had been at the grocery store, Tiffany had birthed her first lamb. I could see that lamb now, tiny, but up and walking. Unfortunately, the lamb had walked away from her mother, and was now firmly trapped inside the wire mesh feeder that we used for the sheep in the winter.

Lambs usually get up and are walking within a few minutes of their birth. They head right away to their mother's side, because, after standing up, their next duty in life is to nurse. Their mother's first milk is a thick, creamy substance called "colostrum". I prefer to call it "Super Juice", because I have seen it revive lambs who were almost dead, and turn them into dynamos after just one small dose.

I immediately realized that this little lamb who was stuck in the feeder may not have had a chance to nurse yet. If a lamb doesn't nurse within a half hour or so of birth, depending on the severity of the weather and its own relative level of strength, it can run out of energy and die. It was, therefore, obvious why this young ewe mother was frantic when she found herself separated from her new lamb.

I lifted the little ewe lamb out of the feeder and set her beside her mother. Immediately, she headed for her mother's side, and was soon nursing eagerly. Peace was restored. I headed back toward the house to take my groceries inside, but I kept thinking of how Tiffany had come and had called to me for help. I had certainly dropped everything to go to her aid. I wondered later how it was that I was so certain I knew what she was saying to me.

Another time I was not so quick to understand a call for help. I had been out in the barnyard, repairing fences. This is a job that has to be done every spring after the winter snows, and after the freezing and thawing cycles are over.

My sheep were all out in a small pasture near the barnyard, or at least that is what I thought. Suddenly a ewe named Heidi came out from the southeast entrance of the barn, walked up to where I was working, and said something to me that sounded like......"Baa,Baa,Baa".

Then she turned around and walked back into the barn. I kept on working on the fences, wondering aloud what that had been all about.

In a little while, Heidi reappeared, walked over to me and again called, "Baa,Baa,Baa". Then she turned and went back into the barn.

"Whoa", I said to myself, "this is a little strange". The ewe looked perfectly fine, however, and since I was making good progress on the fence, I kept on working. I did wonder a little why she wasn't out in the pasture with the rest of the flock.

When Heidi reappeared in a few minutes, and for the third time addressed me directly with, "Baa,Baa,Baa", I was curious enough to follow her as she returned to the barn.

When I walked through the southeast doorway and followed her around the aisles in the old dairy parlor, I found, to my astonishment, that there was another sheep there, lying on the floor. That sheep was obviously very sick.

I raced to her and began trying to attend to her need. Heidi, her friend, who had come repeatedly to fetch me, stood close by watching us.

I was very touched by this experience. All the other sheep were out in the pasture. Heidi had obviously stayed behind with her sick friend, and had also obviously come, not once, but three times to summon me to help.

I had not understood immediately what she was doing, but she had not given up until her cries had been answered, and I had come.

Many people think that animals, especially sheep, are rather dumb. This experience seemed to show me differently. Heidi knew that I was her shepherd, and that I could help her friend. She also cared enough for her friend to stay with her, and was persistent enough to keep calling to me until I responded.

Heidi proved be to a lot smarter than I had given sheep credit for being. I learned from that experience that sheep can be both kind and smart. I decided that I would have to pay more attention to what they were trying to tell me in the future. In my preoccupation with my own tasks, I had almost missed a very important life saving call for help, even though the call sounded a great deal like "Baa,Baa,Baa,"

Chapter 5: <u>Drac, the Sheep Dog</u>

Almost everyone likes to brag about his or her pets, so you'll understand why I want to tell you that I had an amazing sheep dog named Drac. Anybody who knew him still agrees that he was one dog in a million.

His name was pronounced "Drake", but was actually a short version of a long Latin phrase which meant, roughly, "Silver Dragon". He was my older son's white German Shepherd. When my son left home, Drac, rather by default, became my dog.

Around the world, many shepherds enjoy the help of a dog. Some of my shepherd friends favored Border collies, and to be certain, those dogs do work miracles with sheep. They are great at rounding sheep up, at moving them where they should go, even through small gates, and at cutting out individual sheep for the shepherd's attention.

Still, Border Collies work on signals from the shepherd, and, from my observation, they seem to have a hard time relaxing when the job is done. I've heard stories, for example, of Border Collies who always herded the shepherd's children or visitors, or ducks, or anything they could find, when they weren't herding sheep.

Drac was not like that. He was very relaxed. Often he lay quietly right among the sheep, and sometimes I saw sheep licking Drac's face, or touching him, nose to nose, as they greeted one other. The sheep knew that they did not need to be afraid of him.

When it was time to move the sheep from one place to another, I simply TOLD Drac what I wanted him to do. He then circled the flock, and in his deep baritone voice, he TOLD the sheep what he wanted them to do. They always promptly obeyed him, but as soon as the move was over, dog and sheep settled back again into just "hanging out" together.

Drac was an elegantly beautiful dog, fond of soaring effortlessly over fences and other barriers. He had a supremely dignified manner, and made it his business to be wherever I was, whenever he could be. His service to me as a shepherd dog was invaluable, and his friendship is still deeply treasured in memory.

Our pasture lands were situated to the north side of our farm, and our alfalfa hay field lay to the south. Toward the end of each summer, when grass in the pasture got a bit sparse, the sheep began to look longingly toward the alfalfa, still green and growing in that southern hay field.

Alfalfa can grow enormously long roots. Even when everything else is dried up, alfalfa is likely to remain green, because those roots can go down deep into the soil, where the water is.

Sometimes, in their quest for better food, the sheep broke out of the pasture fence for a joyful romp in the young alfalfa. I had a problem keeping them inside the pasture during the fall of the year, especially in years of drought.

Whenever the sheep escaped to the hay field, it was my job, of course, to see that they didn't became bloated from eating too much rich, fresh alfalfa. On those occasions, I simply opened the pasture gate, and then it was Drac's job to go down into the hay field to get them. Drac could be quite convincing, as he ranged back and forth behind them, never too fast, never hostile, but singing out as he went.

In a few minutes, the sheep were usually returned to their pasture, and order was restored. Dare I say it, the flock, now back inside the pasture fence, looked rather "sheepish" for having been caught again in a repeated misdeed.

Once, in early fall, I was headed to the Post Office, hoping to make it before the mail dispatch for that day. As I left the house, I noticed that the sheep were down in the hay field again. "Oh drat it all." I said. "When I get back from the post office I will have to put those sheep back where they belong."

I opened the pasture gate, and then hurried to my car for the short trip to the Post Office. When I returned home a few minutes later, I was quite surprised to find that the sheep were already grazing contentedly INSIDE the pasture fence. Drac came running to meet me from his sentry post, just outside the still open gate.

"Well, I'll be darned!" I said to myself. "He went and got those sheep without me." I patted his head and thanked him for being such a good friend.

People who knew Drac were amazed at how much he understood. For example, if I were going to the grocery store, just down the road, I would say, "Drac, I'm going to the store, and I will be right back."

He then lay down in the driveway. He waited for me to return.

If I told him, however, that I was going off the Island to town, and that I wouldn't be back until evening, he sighed and plopped down on the porch, making no attempt to disguise his displeasure with my plans. Maybe it was just my tone of voice, but he obviously understood the difference between my being "right back", and "not until evening".

Drac was the sort of dog a person could sit and talk to. He patiently listened to me when I had troubles, and tried to comfort me when I was sad. I tried to return the favor and to comfort him when thunder storms boomed overhead. For some reason, Drac was really afraid of thunderstorms.

One Sunday evening I had told him casually that I was going up to church for a song service. I told him I would be home in a little while. He went and lay down on the porch to wait for me.

The church was at the top of a hill, about a quarter mile north of the farm. After services that evening a friend invited us over for some ice cream. I never gave a thought to Drac until a thunder storm came up while we were at our friend's house. I hoped that poor old Drac would not be too upset by the storm, but I didn't worry much about it after all.

When I got home, however, Drac was nowhere to be seen. I called for him, but got no response. Then I did begin to feel somewhat worried. Had he become so upset by the storm that he had run away? I went to bed troubled, but thinking "Oh well, he knows his way around. He will be back by morning."

In the morning, however, there was no Drac to be seen anywhere. "Hm...that's strange", I thought. I went outside and called for him, but he did not come. "He never leaves the farm without me. Where could he have gone?" I asked myself. I recall feeling increasingly anxious as the morning wore on and he did not appear.

Shortly before noon the phone rang. It was a woman calling from a house near the church. She said, "Do you have a large white German Shepherd dog?"

"Oh yes, I do," I replied.

"Well," she said, "He is sitting here on the front steps of the church. Some of the women have come to work in the kitchen, and he won't let anyone go past him into the building. Could you come to get him?"

"Yes, yes, I'll be right there!"

I was flabbergasted! Drac had gone to the church, no doubt, when the storm came, because I had told him that was where I would be. Furthermore, he seemed to have believed I was still there, and he had sat outside the building all night long and half the next day, waiting for me to come out.

When I arrived at the church, he saw me and came running to meet me. His tail wagged, but he had a quizzical look on his face as if to say, "Where were you? You told me you would be at the church. I've been waiting for you."

I felt embarrassed and apologetic. I honestly had no idea that Drac knew where the church was. My telling him where I was going had been done just out of habit. I actually had no notion that he would reckon with what I had said, but obviously he had. There he was, at the church, just where I said I would be.

We got in the truck and drove home. I decided that in the future I would have to take into account the possibility that Drac knew a lot more about what I was saying to him than I could have imagined. I would have to watch what I said.

Chapter 6: <u>Drac (and Spot)</u>

Drac always slept on the kitchen floor, in the corner opposite the wood stove. Although he's been gone for many years now, I can still close my eyes and, in my imagination, see him lying there with his front paws crossed, watching everything that happened around him.

It was to this same kitchen that I always brought newborn lambs if they needed special attention. For several years running we had cold winters, with temperatures dropping below -20 degrees for long stretches of time.

Lambs being born in those temperatures were particularly at risk. During those cold winters, a sizable number of newborns found their way to our kitchen for an emergency "warm up" before they were returned, if possible, to their mothers in the barn.

Right from the beginning, Drac took a lively interest in those needy lambs. I don't mean he just looked at them. He got involved!

We were all remarkably impressed when Drac began the preening routine he'd seen the ewes do with their young. He licked the little creatures from head to tail, and hovered over them as they struggled to get up and walk.

If they ended up having to stay overnight in the house, because their mothers couldn't or wouldn't take them back, Drac took over the mothering duties. In the morning we'd find that he had moved closer to the warmth of the wood stove to sleep, and that the lambs were curled up between his legs, the way a mother dog would shelter her puppies. What an amazing dog!

Now I named this story, Drac and Spot, because Drac wasn't the only dog on the farm. It is time that I introduce you to Spot.

Spot was my husband's dog. He was a mix of Labrador and Chesapeake retrievers, with, I was told by the folks who gave him to us, a bit of Beagle mixed in. He looked like a squat, heavy set Labrador Retriever, but I don't want to insult the breed by claiming that they look like Spot. Whatever the source, Spot was a bit of a misfit.

Even his name was my husband's joke. Spot was all black, with no spots at all, but my husband said that the **whole dog** was a black spot, hence the name. Although I tried to be gracious to Spot and to appreciate his good points, I came to agree with that statement. Spot WAS a black spot, in more ways than one.

He had been trained and disciplined in the same strict manner as had been any other dog we'd ever had, but Spot did not respond to training. He did not care to obey, and so he did not obey.

He did not care whether or not he pleased us. As my father used to say, Spot "took his half out of the middle", meaning that he was selfish. He wanted lots of attention, but gave very little respect in return.

Spot thought all the food in the house was meant for him. Once he climbed up on a chair so he could reach the kitchen table. He then ate three complete cookie sheets full of unbaked hot cross buns, which I had left to rise before baking them in the oven.

When I discovered his thievery, I imagined that he would become very sick from having eaten all that raw yeast dough. Actually he did burp a little more than usual for a day or so, but he was a very durable dog, and his gluttony seemed to affect him very little. I, on the other hand, was furious to have to begin my bread making all over again.

Our dogs were allowed in the house, but they were not allowed to sit or lie on the furniture. Spot obeyed the rule when we were watching him, but every time we left home there was evidence, when we got back, that a certain black dog had taken a nap on our antique couch. Black dog hairs were visible all over the light blue velvet!

You get the picture!

Drac got along well with Spot, although the two were as "different as day and night." Drac had work to do, and Spot was primarily always on the lookout for some self serving opportunity.

One particular day Spot brought out a side of Drac I'd never seen before. It started when Spot just kind of sauntered into the kitchen to see what was going on there.

Drac was very busy looking after two cold lambs I had just brought in from the barn. I was warming up sheep colostrum, the "first milk", which I always kept frozen for emergency lamb "jump starts".

Drac was standing in front of the wood stove, licking first one cold little lamb and then the other. They were lying stretched out on the floor, alive, but barely.

I noticed that Spot meandered over next to Drac, and proceeded to begin licking one of the lambs himself. "Hm...", I mused, "he thinks it must be something good, and he doesn't want to miss out."

Suddenly the most frightening sound I have ever heard emitted from somewhere in Drac's throat. It was a deep, gurgling growl; a most menacing sound, and the meaning was very clear, even to Spot. Drac was saying, "GET AWAY! DON' T YOU EVEN THINK ABOUT IT!"

The normally swaggering Spot started backing nervously away toward the dining room doorway, where he turned and disappeared quickly into the front of the house. Drac continued licking the lambs.

"Hm", I thought, "I would really hate to have Drac angry at me." This normally gentle dog, who allowed small children to clamber over him and to pull his ears, had laid down the gauntlet for Spot when it came to sharing in the care of "his" lambs. Spot was himself a large, heavy dog, but he now knew well enough not to challenge the older dog when Drac had work to do.

There are working dogs and there are "free loading" dogs. As you can see, we had one of each.

When I think of Drac, I always recall one story which, for reasons you will soon see, tops all the others in my estimation. It still makes me pause in wonder!

My neighbor to the south was an elderly, bachelor farmer who kept dairy cows and goats. His name was Carroll, and he called me on the phone everyday, just to visit. He had read many books and was quite knowledgeable about many subjects. I enjoyed our talks.

One day, however, he called to ask if I could bring my dog to help him get his cows back into their pasture. The cows had escaped and had gone back over the hill. He needed my help, well, really, he needed Drac's help get them back.

Drac and I left immediately to meet him. Walking south and then west, we soon found my neighbor and his cows. When Carroll walked ahead to open the pasture gate for us, Drac and I were left behind with the herd, moving them slowly across a wide open hay field.

Carroll had neglected to tell me that one of his cows had "dropped" or birthed a calf just that morning. This explains why I had no warning when suddenly one of his cows turned around and started coming back my way. She naturally and strongly objected to leaving her newborn calf behind in the hay field, but, of course, I didn't even know she had a new calf.

I will tell you that I became very alarmed and then, frankly, terrified, when she began to charge directly at me. ""Oh, my goodness!" I said to myself. "Mother always told me that a charging cow is much more dangerous than is a charging bull."

A bull puts his head down when he charges, and a quick witted person can at times be able to side step to avoid him. A cow keeps her head up as she runs, so she can, therefore, be very, very dangerous. I was now frantically trying to think of what I could do to save myself from this charging cow?

I was in the middle of a large open field. I could not possibly outrun her. She was bearing directly down on me and was closing fast.

In a move born of desperation, I summoned all of my courage and began waving my arms out wide, up and down, and yelling as loudly as I could. I hoped to frighten her with my attempted counter attack.

This all seemed to have no affect whatsoever on the charging cow. She just kept coming. As she drew closer and closer, I numbly resigned myself to the fact that I was about to be very badly hurt, at best.

All at once, I saw a white streak enter my view from the right. Barking, nipping, backing away, Drac had entered the fray like a White Knight on horseback. It brings tears to my eyes even now to recall how masterfully he drew the cow's attention to himself and away from me.

Seeing my chance for escape, I raced for the woods far to my left. I slid behind the first big tree I came to and turned to watch the Wonder Dog in action, still out there in the middle of the big hay field. Drac was barking and feigning. The cow was determined to have her way.

I have no trouble at all admitting that I was gasping and crying, thinking of what a close call I'd just had, and of how much I owed my "Silver Dragon" friend.

Drac eventually turned the cow and continued moving the herd across the field by himself. I walked parallel to them, along the edge of the woods, until the cows were safely inside the pasture and Carroll had closed the gate.

Then I ran to Drac and knelt down, hugging him, while he licked my face. "Thank you, thank you, thank you, dear Drac! I owe my life to you, my friend! Whatever would have become of me if you hadn't run in front of that cow to save me?"

Drac knew what he had done, but he didn't seem to think it at all so extraordinary. After all, he loved me. That was just the kind of thing one does for a friend.

Chapter 7: <u>Tragedies</u>

When my little lamb, "Switch", died the first year I kept sheep, I was very sad. Having a flock of sheep was a childhood dream come true. I thought that bad things weren't supposed to happen in the middle of "sweet" dreams.

Even after I had accepted the loss of Switch, I still clung foolishly to the idea that "from now on" everything else about this dream was going to be wonderful. After all, I'd reasoned, the rest of the lambs who were born that year had done just fine. Perhaps, if I were a very careful and a very attentive shepherd, I should never have to lose another lamb.

That was a nice thought, but it wasn't reality. Soon it became quite apparent that there could, and would, be other disasters to deal with, no matter how hard I tried to avoid them. I found I somehow had to learn to deal with those inevitable losses.

For example, sometimes when I got up in the middle of the night and went to the barn, I found that I had gotten there just a few minutes too late to revive a weak lamb, or to bring it safely out of the cold winter air into the warm kitchen. Instead of rejoicing over a rescue, I had to dispose of a dead lamb. It happened that way occasionally.

Sometimes I just couldn't be there to help a ewe deliver her lambs. In fact, it began to seem to me as if the sheep themselves were working against me. After having read a book that told how sheep and deer and other such animals can actually stop their labor if they are being pursued by predators, I became convinced that some of my ewes deliberately held off going into labor until I had turned off the lights and had gone back into the house. It was as if they did not want me hovering over them while they were having their lambs.

The problem was, however, that if they ran into trouble, where was I? I was sleeping soundly, of course, just across the house yard from them. Their desire to "go it alone" worked against my efforts to help them. Because of that I lost some more lambs.

Then there were accidents, and sometimes there would be illnesses. At those times, I might not lose just lambs. I lost adult sheep too. That was very hard for me.

Sometimes these tragedies were a result of my own lack of vigilance or knowledge. I soon realized that no matter how much I studied my books and tried to prepare for every eventuality, there were any number of things which simply were not covered in those books.

For example, one year my husband and I were planning to attend a friend's wedding in Malaysia. It was very exciting to plan for this long trip, but it meant that I would be away from home right in the middle of the lambing season. I would have to find somebody else to look after my sheep while I was away.

Our daughter and son-in-law agreed to come to help me, but they had no experience at all with sheep, and here I was, leaving them at the most critical time of the year. My shepherd friends could advise them, but since it was also lambing time for them, they were going to be too busy to spend a lot of time at my house.

In an effort to make work easier for my helpers, I asked the farmer who baled my hay that year to make me large round bales, instead of the smaller square bales he usually made. That way, my substitute shepherds could use our tractor to bring feed to the sheep, instead of having to haul it by hand. One large bale would last several days. I reasoned that this would make it easier for them to help me. I could not have been more wrong.

So it was that while we were half way around the world in Malaysia, things were going very badly at home. The lambs, who had been born on schedule and who had seemed to be doing just fine, suddenly began dying, one right after the other. Not just a couple of lambs died, but many of them.

This was obviously very upsetting to our children. They had hoped everything would go well in our absence. Instead, through no fault of their own, they were losing lambs right and left, and did not know why. Neither did any of our shepherd friends.

When we returned from our trip and learned of this great tragedy, I felt very sad. I felt sad because of losing the lambs, but I felt even worse that our kind family had had such a bad experience while trying to be helpful to me.

What I learned later was that big hay bales, sitting out in the field all winter long, can develop molds in among the layers of hay. These molds are not typically harmful to adult sheep, or to cattle, who are often fed with big round bales. I learned too late, however, that the toxins in those molds can be very harmful to little lambs. As soon as my lambs were old enough to begin nibbling moldy hay from those bales with their mothers, they became sick and died. My great idea to save labor for my family had cost them a lot of anguish, and it had cost me the lives of many lambs.

Another year I bought a handsome registered ram in the fall. He had a good temperament and fit in well with the flock. As always, I was looking forward to lambing time. When his lambs began to be born in late winter, however, it was immediately apparent that something was terribly wrong.

Many of them were born with deformed legs. For some it was a mild deformity, but for some it was quite severe. What a pitiful thing it was to see a poor baby lamb so crippled it could never get up to walk!

Obviously, I could not keep any of the lambs that year, not even the ones who appeared to be fine. I was concerned that even they might be carriers for the deformity and that in the future this could have resulted in their own lambs' being born deformed.

Neither could I ever use that ram to father more lambs. A whole year's effort, and the price of a registered ram, were lost because of an invisible flaw in his genes; something I could not have known in advance.

The worst tragedy of all occurred one summer when some older children visited our farm. They went outside to play, and, without my knowing it, left a door open which led from the barnyard to the granary, where we stored our grain. Eventually my sheep found the "door left open". They went inside and found all the corn and oats they could ever hope to eat.

Those sheep must have thought they were in heaven. They loved grain, and so they couldn't stop themselves. They ate and ate and ate. They ate way, way too much!

When we humans eat something bad for us, we can do something unpleasant, but actually very helpful. We can vomit, or "throw up" the bad food we have eaten, and thus get rid of it. We don't have to stay sick.

Sheep cannot vomit! Their stomachs are divided into four separate chambers. Once that grain goes in, it stays in!

After eating all that grain my sheep became terribly, terribly sick. The grain in their stomachs began to swell as it mixed with their digestive juices, and it began to emit gases. Soon the sheep's stomachs were stretched tightly by the swelling grain and gases.

When I finally discovered that the door to the granary had been left open, and that the sheep had gotten in to gorge themselves, it was already too late. Several of my strongest and most productive sheep were deathly sick.

We did not have a veterinarian close by, nor an old shepherd who knew how to do the necessary surgery to relieve the pressure. I did all I could to try to save my sheep. I fed them mineral oil and soda water in an attempt to help them to pass the grain. In spite of my efforts, seven of my sheep died, and they died in absolute misery and suffering.

I was distraught at my loss. These sheep had been my friends. How could they have been so foolish as to have eaten themselves to death?

I knew by this time that it was useless to mourn my losses, but I did so anyway. I also knew that I couldn't be angry at the visiting children. These children were from the city, and unlike farm children, they had not been raised to have very strong habits of shutting every door or gate they ever opened. They did not know any better. They had just been curious to see what was in the barn.

As a result of this tragedy, I determined to be more careful than ever. I even put a lock on the granary door. That made it less convenient for me to come and go, but it made it much safer for the sheep.

So, as my years as a shepherd went by, I experienced an ongoing blending of delightful events and untimely tragedies. Somewhere along the way I began to notice something rather amazing about my sheep. I noticed that when a lamb died, the mother sheep seemed to be able to accept the loss of her own newborn more peacefully than I did.

When there were very sad experiences, such as the death of seven ewes at one time, I could see that the surviving sheep always seemed to be able to carry on, without spending much time in mourning.

At first it seemed to me as if the sheep didn't have any awareness or feelings about their loss. Some people say that sheep are very dumb. Maybe they are right!

With experience, I learned that this was not the case at all. The sheep were actually very much aware of the bad things which happened to the other members of the flock. They had a serenity about it, however, which, I have to admit, I did not have.

Eventually I allowed the sheep to teach me what they knew. I learned that the most valuable response I can have to bad experiences is to accept the reality of the present bad situation, and to remain hopeful for the future. I had started out asking for a magical experience in raising sheep. I ended up having a growing experience instead.

Chapter 8: <u>Arlington</u>

I grew up in the 1940's and 50's in rural Western Pennsylvania, in the midst of farms and forests, streams and wildlife. My parents taught my brothers and me a lot about the nature which surrounded us. Maybe that fact helped to make biology one of my favorite subjects at school.

I was especially fascinated with the study of genetics. That is the part of biology which explains why some of my dog's puppies were brown and some were black, and why some had short hair while others had curly hair. Though a great deal more is known about genetics now than when I went to school, even then, I found learning about genetics to be just wonderful.

After I had kept sheep for several years, I became very excited when I heard that the University of Wisconsin was experimenting with sheep genetics. I tried to learn all I could about it.

Their experiment was with the Booroola Merino sheep breed, originally developed in Australia. Standard Merino sheep are known worldwide for their excellent wool, but the Booroola Merino sheep are famous for the fact that they are very prolific. Booroola Merino ewes almost always have at least twins, and often deliver three, four, or sometimes even five or six lambs at a time.

This is unheard of among most other breeds. Of course, you can see that if a farmer had five lambs to sell from each ewe every year, it would be more profitable than if each ewe had just one or two lambs.

The University of Wisconsin's experiment was aimed at trying to learn if the tendency to have many lambs was a characteristic which could be passed on when the Booroola Merinos were cross bred with other sheep. Could my Columbia sheep, for example, be bred to Booroola Merinos and still retain the Columbia characteristics, while also attaining the Booroola Merino tendency to have many lambs.

What made me excited about the university's project was that ordinary farmers in Wisconsin were invited to take part in the experiment. The scientists at the Arlington Agricultural Research Station, University of Wisconsin-Madison were selling young Booroola Merino crossbred ram lambs to the public at rather low prices. They were doing this in order to expand their genetics experiment beyond the capacity of the Sheep Research Station.

I quickly called up, signed up and was accepted to receive a ram. Then I drove my pickup truck to Arlington, Wisconsin. There I selected a young ram lamb whose sire, that is, his father, had been a Booroola Merino. His dam, that is, his mother, on the other hand, had been a Dorset ewe.

Dorset ewes are well known for being excellent mothers. Standard Dorsets, like Merinos, are also known for having large curling horns. Hm…I liked that "good mother" part, but those horns looked dangerous. My Columbia sheep were very large, but had no horns and were very gentle.

Still, I couldn't resist being a part of this genetics project. I bought a Booroola Merino/Dorset cross ram lamb, and took him home with me to Washington Island. I named my new ram, aptly, "Arlington", after the University of Wisconsin's Arlington Sheep Research Station.

Arlington adjusted well to his new home, and to all of his new sheep companions. I was happy to have him, and looked forward to learning more about genetics.

I must try to make you understand that I was going to have to wait a long time to learn the results of any experiment with Arlington. First, I would have to wait until Arlington had sired daughters. Since it was summer when I bought Arlington, it would take several months before any of his daughters would be born.

Then I would have to wait until Arlington's daughters grew old enough to have lambs of their own. That could likely take another two years. Only then would I see how many of them had multiple lambs, instead of a single or twins.

Then, of course, I would have to wait still longer to see how any multiple lambs grew, and whether or not their mothers could take care of so many. Counting up all the waiting, it could be well over three years before I would see any results from the experiment with Arlington's genetics.

My, that was certainly going to be a lot of waiting, but, hey, I knew how to wait patiently. I'd waited all the way from childhood to middle age adulthood to own sheep. I could afford to wait a few more years to learn the answers to my genetics questions.

Meanwhile, I watched Arlington grow and grow. The part I watched most carefully were those heavy curling horns.

Hm…I reasoned that those horns could do a lot of damage if Arlington ever decided to be nasty. I wasn't exactly comfortable about that part of the experiment.

Unfortunately, as time went on my fears about Arlington were indeed confirmed. During his first winter I began to notice that he was not quite the gentleman my Columbia rams had always been. In fact, as he grew bigger, he began to be quite bossy and pushy.

He had those horns to enforce his will. When he decided he wanted to eat from the feeder, he banged into any ewe who may have already been eating there, in order to make her move. He did this, even though other spaces were open at the feeder.

I watched this behavior with growing alarm. Any farmer will tell you that temperament in animals is not something you can train away. If a ram is going to be mean and nasty, there is nothing one can do to change him. The worst part about this is that if he is mean and nasty, it is also a real possibility that his offspring will tend to be mean and nasty too.

Rams are typically penned up and isolated from the ewe flock for most of the year. During breeding season, of course, which is roughly from August through December, the ram runs with the ewe flock. After seeing how Arlington was behaving, I knew that right after the breeding season I would have to pen Arlington up by himself. I had never had to do that with my gentle Columbia rams.

I began to wonder if my love of studying genetics were not about to get me into trouble. Had I made a wrong choice in buying Arlington? My answer came soon enough.

One snowy morning in late November, I was putting hay bales out into the feeders in the barnyard. I always carried an old kitchen knife with me in order to cut the baler twine that ties up the hay. Fortunately, I had the knife with me this particular morning.

As I shook the hay into the feeder, I was suddenly struck violently from behind. I was knocked off my feet and thrown to the ground. The knife went flying out of my hand. I landed hard on my shoulder and side. Thankfully, I was not seriously injured.

As I scrambled to my feet, I turned and tried to spot my attacker. There was Arlington, standing a few yards away from me. Apparently he had not been content just to send me flying, because he now began backing up slowly to make another run at me.

Unconsciously I reached back into my childhood training and the lessons of my family's farming experience. I knew I had to make a choice right away. I could run for the fence, and possibly I could make it to safety before Arlington managed to get to me again. The down side of that choice, however, was that he would then believe he could get away with attacking me again in the future.

The other choice was riskier, but perhaps would have the better long term outcome. I chose it instead!

I saw the old knife lying on the ground beside me. I scooped it up. Holding it in my gloved hand by the blade end, I advanced rapidly toward Arlington with the heavy wooden handle exposed.

I yelled at him at the top of my voice. "DON'T you even think of it!!!!" I cried out as I rushed toward him. My arm was raised with the intent to strike him.

That armor plate on the top of his head was thick and tough. I knew better than to hit him there, but about eight inches down his face, below that armor, was his tender nose.

Before he even had a chance to change intention or direction, I closed the gap between us and began landing my knife handle on his nose repeatedly. He was so surprised at the sudden change of initiative that he just stood there stupefied for a moment. I kept screaming at him and kept up the barrage on his nose.

I did not want really to harm him, but I did most certainly want him to feel pain. I knew if I didn't show him that I was the boss, and if I didn't do that decisively, he would only become ever more aggressive toward me. This could not be allowed!

Arlington retreated to the far corner of the barnyard with his head hung low. He looked to be considering his options. Finally, he just walked slowly back to the feeder and began to eat with the ewes, who, amazingly enough, had continued munching contentedly throughout this whole episode.

While I caught my breath and brushed myself off, I also considered my own options. Because of his genetic attributes, Arlington was potentially a very valuable ram. He had just demonstrated, however, that his aggressive temperament was a serious liability and a threat to me.

I would have to get rid of him! I could not afford to risk my own safety, or the safety of my many visitors, just because he was a "valuable" ram.

I also realized, however, that my being located on an isolated island at the beginning of winter meant that my options for replacing him right now were limited.

My compromise decision was that I would keep him through the remainder of this breeding season. Then, genetic marvel or not, I would try to sell him to somebody else who was more equipped than I to handle him.

I felt sad, because I liked Arlington, or at least I HAD liked Arlington before he attacked me. Now, no matter what potential help he could have been to my sheep business, the fact that I could not trust him cancelled out his positive attributes.

From that day on, until I sold Arlington the next spring, I NEVER went into the barnyard for any reason without having my old kitchen knife in my hand and clearly in his view.

Arlington always watched me out of the corner of his eye. I don't know what he was thinking, but I imagined that he was remembering his stinging nose. At least I hoped that was what he was remembering.

Arlington never again attacked me, but you can be certain that I also never again turned my back on him either. Once in a while he would start backing up as if he had in mind to rush me. At those times I would show him the knife handle and would yell at him, "DON'T you even think of it!!!" and he would stand down.

It was a great relief, that next spring, when a truck pulled out of our driveway with Arlington in the back. "Goodbye, Arlington!" I called. "Be careful, Mr. Farmer!"

I started out this story by telling you that I would have to be patient in order to find out if the Booroola Merino genetics experiment worked. Well, sure enough, the same spring I sold Arlington, his ewe lambs began to be born.

When they were two years old, they began having lambs of their own. Boy, did they have lambs; three, four, and a couple of times, five at a time. The genetic experiment had obviously worked, but guess what? Those Arlington daughters, who had indeed inherited the Booroola Merino tendency to have many lambs, had also inherited their father's undesirable temperament.

They were aggressive with the other ewes, and they were miserable failures as mothers. Sometimes they never even bothered to lick off their newborns. Sometimes they just abandoned them where they lay.

I was accustomed to my wonderful, attentive Columbia ewes. I knew that Arlington's Dorset mother was from a breed known to be good mothers too. His nasty "attitude", which passed on to his daughters, must have come from somewhere. I don't want to blame the Booroola Merino breed, when Arlington is the only example I have to judge them by. Perhaps Arlington was just a "bad apple" in a good bushel.

In any case, I do know that my genetic experiment succeeded. The flock had many, many lambs from Arlington's daughters, but because his daughters were such poor mothers, the only ones of their lambs who thrived were the ones I took away from them at birth, and fed with a bottle.

The summer following Arlington's departure from the flock, I bought a new, registered Dorset ram. He had curling horns, but was very gentle, just as my Columbia rams had been.

I kept some of Arlington's granddaughters. After a few more years had gone by, Arlington's great granddaughters and great great granddaughters were still having lots of lambs. These ewes were gentle in temperament and were great mothers, acquiring, it would seem, the good traits from their Dorset and Columbia genes.

When I finally sold my entire flock, the new farmer had the benefit of the genetic experiment without any of the headaches. I do not have the University of Wisconsin's credentials, but I concluded for myself that it is possible for the Booroola Merino multiple birth tendency to be passed on genetically to other breeds of sheep, and, over time, for the positive qualities of those other breeds to be retained.

I had waited years for the results! It was fun to have taken part in the research. In the end, I figured out that all that was really needed for the scientific experiment to be a success had been an abundant supply of patience, and an old kitchen knife with a very heavy wooden handle.

Chapter 9: <u>The Sheep and the Goat</u>

Looking back I can see that it really was all my fault. I simply made one judgment error after another.

It all started one summer when our shepherd friends from the mainland, Mark and Michelle, went on a vacation with their children. They made arrangements for somebody to look after their sheep; not such a hard job when the sheep are out on pasture.

They asked me if I would be willing to look after their goat. "Of course! I'll be glad to", I said, not thinking much about it. I realize now that my first mistake was in not asking more questions about that goat.

Inga was a white Saanen dairy goat. She arrived at our farm early one July morning. I kept her confined in the barn for the first couple of days, in order to allow her get accustomed to her surroundings.

My second mistake in judgment was when I decided to take her out to join my sheep in the pasture. I figured she would be easier to care for if I didn't have to carry food and water to her.

I knew that goats really hate to be alone, so I also thought that she would enjoy the company of the sheep. I wanted to be kind to her. That was my third mistake in judgment.

Inga adapted well to being with the flock. There was no fighting. She stayed with them as they grazed. I soon settled into a false sense of peace and security. I reasoned, "Oh, this will be O.K.. Inga won't be much trouble to care for at all." That conclusion was my fourth mistake in judgment.

All those mistakes in judgment added up to a crisis in the making. I had no way of knowing......

A couple of mornings after Inga joined the flock, I went out to check on the sheep. This was something I did several times a day. The sheep were not in the barnyard. I surmised they had to be in the pasture.

I had eight separate pastures, each of which could be closed off from the others when grass was sparse, and when we needed to manage the sheep's consumption of forage. At the time of Inga's arrival at the farm, however, there was plenty of grass, so all the pasture gates were open and the sheep were free to graze wherever they wanted to.

I stood by the barn and scanned the different pastures, but saw no sheep. I walked out toward the maple grove a bit, but I still couldn't see any of my sheep. "Hmmm......That's strange. Are they all lying down at once? Why can't I see them?"

I circled on foot through the eight pastures. That's how I made a startling discovery. The sheep were not in any of the pastures.

"O.K. They must be in the alfalfa," I concluded. I hadn't seen them there, but then I really hadn't looked, so I wasn't too anxious, yet!

When I checked the hay field, however, they were not there either. Now I began to feel a little panicky. "Where were my sheep? Where had they gone?"

This had never happened before. Sheep are very responsive to the needs of their stomachs. Their travels are most always in response to their hunger. Why, if they had left their pasture, would they also leave the lush hay field. This made no sense at all, but like "Mary" looking for her lost lamb, I was now on a mission.

I began to scan the fields beyond our farm. I looked south, toward Carroll's farm, but the sheep were not there. I looked eastward, toward where my husband's cousin lived. No sheep were in sight there. Mrs. Anderson's field lay to the north, but there were no sheep there. Mr. Hansen's woods were to the west.

"The woods! Could they possibly have gone there or back over the hill?"

I felt comforted by the fact that we live on an island. I knew, in the worst case, they could not leave the Island. Still it is a fairly large island, 35 sq. miles. That is a lot of space to wander through, if they were in the mood to wander.

I cannot tell you what a bad feeling it was to know that my sheep were missing; that they had willfully left my care and had gone off on their own.

"What would they do for water? How would the little ones survive? Would they find their way back?"

Then suddenly I thought about the goat. "The goat! Of course, the goat! They aren't alone after all! Inga is with them. She's led them all off! Why, oh why would they follow her when they have everything they need right here?"

I don't want to offend people who keep goats, but even the most devoted goatherd will admit, "Goats have strong opinions, and they aren't shy about acting on them." I was now thoroughly convinced that Inga had led my flock astray. This was not good at all.

Goats are primarily browsers, who like to eat low growing leaves from shrubs and bushes. Sheep are primarily grazers, who eat grasses and plants that grow close to the ground, but sheep will browse, if they have the opportunity.

If Inga were now in charge of this escapade, she'd likely be heading for the woods, and for fallow fields, full of the brush and shrubs which were more to her liking than were our pasture grasses.

"Oh, no!", I cried, "My sheep will be filthy! Burrs, twigs, seed pods will be all through their wool! What a mess come shearing time." Dirty wool costs more to process and brings a lower price when sold. "Inga, I'm not feeling very kind thoughts about you right now!" I said to myself.

I went and got into my pickup truck and started driving up and down the roads in our neighborhood, hoping to catch a glimpse of the flock. The worst part, in this situation, was that most of the Island to the west of our farm is wooded, and there are very few roads.

I knew that those sheep could be anywhere in those woods. I would not be able to see them from the road. If they were on the move, I could drive around, just missing them by minutes, as I searched in all the wrong places.

After looking along the roadways for a while, I went home and called some of my neighbors on the phone. Perhaps someone I knew had seen them. Unfortunately, nobody had seen anything. There was no helpful information.

After lunch I started out on foot. I'd be so happy if I could tell you that Drac went with me, but my dearest dog friend had died of old age the summer before. On this day I missed his help a lot. I was alone, and feeling very much alone at that.

As the afternoon and my search, wore on, I looked with hope toward the evening. "Surely," I told myself, "the sheep will come home to sleep in the barnyard. Won't they want to come home at evening time?"

I worried a little that they might not be able to find their way home, but then animals really are a lot smarter than most people give them credit for being. I shoved that worrisome thought away.

At sunset, after tramping through the woods all afternoon, it was only I who came home tired and weary that day. Through the night I checked the barn over and over again, but no sheep appeared any time.

I tried to sleep, but I felt so bad about my sheep's being "out there in the woods somewhere", that I couldn't sleep. For years I had gone to bed each night, listening to the low noises they made in the barn. Now it was very, very quiet.

Being a shepherd is a little like being a mother. I've been both, so I can make the comparison. Like a watchful mother is with her children, a true shepherd ALWAYS has one ear cocked, and one eye tilted toward the sheep. Because I was a shepherd whose sheep were now missing, I could scarcely think of anything else. I was very anxious about them.

The next morning I checked the barn and again found it empty. I began my search of the roads again. My elderly friend, Myra, asked to go with me in the truck. Myra, admittedly, could not see very well, but she was a great encourager, and I certainly needed encouragement.

This time we drove all over the Island. We drove through narrow woodland lanes where an old pickup truck really shouldn't go. We talked to anybody we saw, asking them if they had seen the sheep. Nobody had seen the flock.

The second day of searching ended with my being totally dejected and terribly worried. The sheep had now been gone for two days. They would have had no water to drink during that time. This was not good!

On the morning of the third day, I hurried out to the barn. I hoped that a miracle had occurred during the night. Perhaps they had come home. I ran through the barn door. No sheep!

Wait, what was this? Why, one sheep, all alone, was standing just inside the nearest enclosure.

"Joey! Joey! What are you doing here?" I cried out. Joey was a yearling ram lamb whom I had raised, with Drac's help, as a "bottle baby".

Wow! This sheep's solitary presence in my barn was a bit of a wonder.

First, he had found his way home alone from wherever that "dratted goat" had taken my sheep. Second, his bond with me as his shepherd had obviously been stronger than his bond with the rest of the flock. It is very rare for a sheep to leave his flock to travel anywhere on his own.

I know I am using my imagination, to be certain, but I felt as if Joey had made an independent decision. He had defied the "law of the flock", and the evil spell of that goat, and he had come home by himself. Perhaps he had reasoned that things out there in the wild were just not right. Perhaps he had come to find me.

However Joey had gotten out of the pasture, he had somehow gotten himself back in. Perhaps he could now lead me to the others.

"Joey", I said, "Oh dear, Joey. I am so glad to see you. Where are the others? Can you take me to them?"

I opened the gate, and Joey stepped right through to meet me. I knelt down and hugged his neck and scratched his ears. Then we walked together through the barn door into the house yard. We walked side by side around the barnyard fence, and into the hay field to the south of the barn.

"O.K., Joey," I said. "Take me to the flock."

Joey started off across the hayfield, moving briskly. I stayed just at his left flank. It felt strange to be walking side by side with a sheep. Drac and I had often walked together like this, but this was Joey, a supposedly "dumb animal".

He led me to the gap in the stone fence between my hay field and my neighbor, Carroll's, hay field to the south. Then we headed west, back toward the woods, then south, and west again. Joey led me to the far end of Carroll's long narrow field. We entered the woods and headed north.

Suddenly Joey stopped and looked all around him. He seemed puzzled.

"Poor Joey," I said, "They've moved again, haven't they, fellow? This is where they were, but they aren't here now. "

We stood together for a moment. Joey had done his amazing best. I'm convinced he took me to where the sheep had been when he had left them, but they were nowhere to be seen now.

"I'm sorry, Joey. You did your best, and I thank you for that. Let's go on home now."

By this time we were about three quarters of a mile from the house. Joey and I retraced our steps, south, east, north, and east again toward our hay field. Just as we were about to cross back through the gap in the stone boundary fence between Carroll's farm and ours, I glanced north and west toward Mr. Hansen's woods. For a moment I thought I had seen a flash of white there at the edge of the underbrush.

"Let's go have a look, Joey."

We headed northwest. Sure enough, even though I had searched those woods many times before, this time the sheep were there.

As we approached, they looked up from their browsing and called either to me or to one another. And yes, there was that "dratted goat", Inga, at the lead end of the flock.

"O.K. Ladies. Recess is over. It's time to go home."

I circled behind them, clapping my hands. They began to line up for the walk back to the barnyard.

In the actual presence of their shepherd, the evil spell of the wayward goat seemed to lie broken. My flock was again responsive to my good will for them, and maybe they were thirsty enough to want the safety and provision of their own barnyard. In any case, Joey had helped to find them after all, and soon they were all back home again, acting as if nothing at all unusual had happened.

Inga, like it or not, was also back in a locked up jail pen, where she stayed until her owners returned. I no longer minded carrying food and water to her. I was just relieved to have the flock home safely again.

When I now recall this misadventure, I think it really is a story about two individuals who provided leadership, albeit quite different in character.

Inga, the goat, somehow had persuaded the entire flock to leave familiar shelter, water, and safety for a dangerous romp in the wild. I suppose we could say that it is the nature of goats to do as she did. I could not despise her for being a normal goat.

Joey, the ram lamb, on the other hand, was the more remarkable. It was not at all normal for him to do what he had done. He not only broke away from the bad influence of the goat, but even more, he overcame all that is normal in the nature of a sheep. He broke with his own flock in order to journey alone to find his shepherd. He somehow believed that I was the only one who could rescue them all. I do still marvel at that, and I admire him for it to this day.

Chapter 10: <u>Cassi, the Wonder Sheep</u>

I should like to be able to tell you that I loved all of my sheep equally, but that is just not true. As it is with people, each individual sheep had his or her own unique personality and exhibited a distinctive character. That means that not all were equally attractive.

For example, there was that little yearling ewe lamb who had managed to jump on the stock truck with the first sheep I bought. I named her Eileen, and she was still alive and productive thirteen years later, when I sold my whole flock.

Eileen was obviously strong, because fourteen years is an awfully long time for a sheep to live. The average life span for a sheep is about the same as for a large dog, that is, ten or eleven years. Eileen even birthed a lamb in her last year with me, which was simply amazing.

When she was young, Eileen was admittedly very beautiful, as sheep beauty goes. She was tall and well formed. She had a straight, strong back, a regal bearing, and thick, lustrous fleece. Her wool grew long and had a highly desirable crimp in each strand, a quality which is prized by hand spinners.

Since we have a famous fiber arts school on our Island, there were always customers eager to buy my best fleeces. For a few years one woman had an exclusive standing order to purchase Eileen's superior fleece each time we sheared.

In addition, Eileen always kept herself meticulously clean. Even when the other sheep got hay or leaves imbedded in their coats, Eileen's fleece was white and free of vegetation. I don't know how she did it, but Eileen always looked as if she were ready for an elegant occasion.

Although she was certainly a grand lady, Eileen did not, however, have a pleasant personality. She somehow seemed to understand that she was beautiful, and that her fleece was extraordinary. She exhibited a haughty spirit. To put it bluntly, Eileen was plainly prideful!

She expected to be first in line, to get the best food and to have the best place to sleep. She would often stamp one of her front feet at me, as a sign of impatience or displeasure, if she thought I were taking too long getting her oats or hay into the winter feeder.

Eileen always cared adequately for her lambs, but she did not seem to enjoy being a mother. None of her lambs ever grew up to be as regal or as beautiful as she was.

You may think I am just imagining this, but ask any small scale farmer who really takes the time to know his or her animals. He or she will agree that each animal is as distinctively individual as are the different children in a teacher's classroom, or the brothers and sisters in a family.

Eileen made me feel amused at times by her consistent, focused appreciation of herself. Beyond that, however, we were not actually the best of friends.

On the other hand, the sheep I did like and admire the most was a ewe whom I had named Cassi. She was born the second year I had the flock. Even as a ewe lamb in her first year, I could see that she was very special.

Cassi was not as elegant in her appearance as was Eileen, but she was gentle and patient. She had a simple, confident dignity that I liked very much.

Cassi birthed not one, but two sets of twins almost every year. That kind of productivity was amazing, and would have earned the gratitude of any farmer. Over her eleven year lifetime, Cassi delivered and raised more lambs than any other ewe I ever had, or ever even heard of.

I respected Cassi most of all because she was such a magnificent mother. Her lambs always grew quickly and were all, like her, pleasant and responsive individuals.

Often I would find Cassi lying down with her lambs curled up and sleeping on her back. There her little ones were kept warm by her thick fleece.

She patiently allowed them to run and jump over her as she rested. It was obvious that her lambs always felt secure and happy.

Cassi seemed to like me too. She would come and touch my hand with her nose when I was walking in the barn. She cooperated when I trimmed her hooves, or gave her medicine to guard against intestinal worms.

As I said, I loved all of my sheep, and cared for them as faithfully as I could, but without question, Cassi was the sheep I felt closest to and admired the most. It seemed as if we were really trusting friends.

Cassi was exceptionally strong and capable. She had given birth alone many times, and never needed help from me. I admit I probably took it for granted that it would always be that way for her. On one memorable occasion, however, it wasn't!

Just as it is with human mothers, the experience of giving birth is one of the most significant times in a ewe's life. It is also one of the most vulnerable times, because things can sometimes go wrong.

During the five months it takes for a lamb to develop before being born, the mother ewe's body grows ever wider until the area right in front of her hip bones becomes very round and full. This is because the lamb, or lambs, are growing bigger and bigger inside the ewe's body.

While a lamb is developing, it is attached to the inside of its mother's uterus at special "button like" places on the uterus wall. I prefer to think of them as electrical outlets, where the lamb's umbilical cord is plugged in.

Through this "outlet" the lamb's body receives nourishment from the mother as it grows. It also has its waste material removed for elimination through the mother's kidneys and bladder.

The shepherd knows approximately when his ewes will deliver their lambs, but it takes a watchful eye to try to know exactly when the lambs will be born. He or she will want to be present, if at all possible, in order to try to prevent unnecessary losses of lambs, or even of ewes. This means there will be ever more frequent visits to the barn or shed, looking for signs as the delivery draws near.

The first sign the shepherd looks for is a change in the shape of the ewe's body. A lamb is supposed to be born head first, with its front hooves extended over its head. This position is much like that of an Olympic diver, about to jump from a platform into a swimming pool.

Just as with a human baby, a lamb shifts its position inside the mother's body a day or so before it is born. At that time, hopefully, it assumes the "Olympic diver" position at the opening of the birth canal in preparation for the onset of labor.

When this change in the lamb's position has occurred, a hollow place just in front of the ewe's hip bones will appear. This will be right at the place which before had been the roundest and fullest.

Then we look for a swelling of the tissue around the opening under the sheep's tail. This is where the lamb will emerge. Usually there will also be a gooey mucus substance which begins to drip out about the same time as the lamb shifts its position in the uterus.

"Labor" is when the ewe's body begins rhythmic contractions in a process which will move the lamb through the birth canal and out of the ewe's body. It is called "labor" because, frankly, it is very hard work for the ewe.

When labor starts, the ewe often moves about in a circle and paws the ground with a front hoof. Sometimes she stands off by herself, away from the other sheep. Sometimes she lowers her head, as if she's sad or is thinking hard about something.

Occasionally she lies down on her side and stretches her neck out as far as she can in one direction. At the same time she stretches her top rear leg as far as she can in the opposite direction. Then she gets up and walks around again.

When a diligent shepherd sees these first signs, he or she becomes ever more watchful. More frequent visits are made to the barn, even in the middle of the night. It is very important for the shepherd to try to be aware of any birthing that is about to take place.

Most ewes deliver their lambs without help from the shepherd. It is best for all concerned if she does. There are fewer chances of infection if the birthing is done by the sheep without assistance. The sheep is also less frightened if she can take care of this important event by herself.

Sometimes, however, the shepherd needs to assist because something unforeseen has gone wrong in the birthing process. For example, if a ewe is carrying twins, or triplets, you can imagine that there are lots of legs and tails and heads which can sometimes get tangled up as the lambs head for the birth canal.

If that tangling up happens, then the lambs cannot make it through the birth canal. The longer the ewe tries in vain to expel her lambs, the more chance the lambs can end up swallowing the amniotic fluid which has cushioned them inside the ewe's uterus. If that happens, they can suffocate before they are even born.

When the shepherd sees that the ewe's labor seems to be going on too long, or if the sheep looks as if she is having too much trouble delivering her lambs, he or she must then intervene to help.

"To help" means that the shepherd carefully washes his or her hands and reaches up inside the sheep's birth canal and into the uterus in order to discover what may be happening inside. Only during labor is the opening to the ewe's uterus large enough for a shepherd's hand to fit inside. The object of this intrusion is to help a lamb, or lambs, move successfully outward, through that same opening, into the world beyond, that is, to be "born".

If the lamb is being pushed forward by the ewe's laboring, but is not in the "Olympic diver's position", it cannot, in most cases, pass through the birth canal. The shepherd must try to "see" with his or her fingers what is happening inside the ewe's body. Then he or she must move the lambs, one at a time, into the correct position to be born.

There is very little space inside a ewe's uterus, especially if the lambs are large. It takes a lot of strength and imagination to move wiggly lambs into position for birth, particularly if they have gotten themselves turned and tangled on the inside.

Both the sheep and the shepherd can be utterly exhausted by the time the birthing is over. If the lambs are saved, however, it is also very exhilarating and rewarding for the shepherd who has offered assistance.

One winter night, when I got up for a routine check on the flock, I was shocked and dismayed to discover that Cassi was in trouble! Lying flat on her side, she lifted her head weakly as I approached. Her look could have said, "Where have you been? I've been needing you."

It appeared to me that she had been in labor for some time and was already quite exhausted. I chastised myself for not having noticed her labor signs before I had gone to bed. I don't know how I could have missed spotting them. The mere thought of my losing Cassi was unbearable. I immediately threw off my coat and flew into action.

"Please, Please don't let me lose Cassi because I wasn't paying close enough attention!" I felt stunned and my heart raced with anxiety.

Cassi had always taken good care of herself before. Maybe that was why I had not been too concerned about her; had not even noticed the signs which must have been there.

This time had obviously been different! I cringed at the thought of my not having been there earlier, when Cassi first needed me. I raced to wash my hands in cold water from the faucet and then knelt by her heaving side.

As I reached my hand inside her, I felt a jumble of legs. There were more than one lamb. I couldn't tell which parts belonged to which lamb, nor could I figure out how they were positioned inside.

My fingers followed a leg up to a body, but my brain couldn't figure out whether that lamb was coming backwards, what we call "breech" delivery, or if both lambs were trying to come through the birth canal at the same time.

I needed desperately to get the puzzle solved quickly! I was very worried, but it seemed the more I tried to figure it out, the more confused I became. I had to talk out loud to make myself slow down, so I could try to "see" what my fingers were feeling.

Finally, it came clear to me. The first lamb was "presenting" as we say, one front leg and its head, but its other front leg was bent away to the back. In that position, the lamb's squared shoulder had made it impossible for it to slip through the birth canal.

In order to get that lamb into the "Olympic diver" position, I would have to push it back through the birth canal into the uterus. Then I would have to reach my fingers around to snag the dragging front leg and pull it into position over the lamb's head.

Pushing back was not so easy, however. Cassi's body was blindly pushing in the opposite direction, and her muscles were still very strong.

I waited for a pause in Cassi's muscle contractions. Then I pushed with all my strength against the presenting lamb's shoulder and chest, shoving it slowly back through the birth canal and into the larger uterus cavity. As soon as I did this, I found another lamb's legs were also tangled up in the mix, and that the second lamb was "presenting" back legs first, or "breech". Oh my! Oh my! This was going to be difficult!

Finally, after a couple of failed attempts, I was able to grab two front legs between my fingers. By sliding my hand up higher, I determined that they belonged to only one lamb. I could feel the lamb's head between its front legs. I pulled the lamb's legs together toward me. Then I tucked its head down, and now, working in time with Cassi's own uterine muscle contractions, I started gently to pull the lamb down and out of the birth canal.

Once everything was in the right position, the birthing was actually quite easy. The lamb slipped out smoothly onto the straw on the barn floor.

I wish so much that I could tell you the lamb was OK, but that is not true. The lamb looked obviously dead.

I tried blowing air into its lungs anyway, through its mouth, while holding its nostrils pinched shut. The raspy rattle I heard told me that too much time had gone by. Its lungs were flooded. The dear little creature had drowned in the amniotic fluid inside the uterus. I felt terrible!

I knew I would likely find the second lamb dead as well. My fingers went back inside the ewe, and I positioned and pulled the second lamb into the light.

I was correct. The second lamb was dead also.

I looked sadly down at two dead lambs and a worn and weary ewe. I had simply not been attentive enough. I had not been present when I was needed.

I was also utterly exhausted from my efforts. I sat still, filthy and wet from having rolled around on the barn floor.

I looked over at Cassi lying in front of me. As she struggled to get up I could see, though she was extremely tired, that it appeared she would be OK after all.

I closed my eyes for a moment, my arms and legs drooping. I just needed to rest for a few moments.

Suddenly I felt something I had never felt before! Cassi had stepped to my side and was licking my face all over.

A ewe always licks its newborn to clean it off. The licking stimulates the lamb's blood circulation and helps it to get ready to stand up and walk. It is essential for the lamb's survival that this be done.

I've seen ewes even lick clean their dead lambs. It seems as if they are determined to carry out their duties, even if there is no hope. Perhaps doing so is a way for them to grieve their loss.

Cassi, however, was ignoring her lambs. She was licking my face! I gasped!

I felt as if Cassi were thanking me for my great effort to help her. We had just been though an ordeal together. We had lost the lambs. They were the only lambs Cassi ever lost in her life, and this was the only time she had ever needed my help in delivery.

Some people might say that I'm wrong; that Cassi was just following her instincts. I can agree that licking her own lambs would have been instinctual, but it certainly was not instinctual for her to be licking me. Nothing like that had ever happened before that I knew of.

I started to cry. It felt as if Cassi were trying to comfort ME, for goodness sake! I felt as if she were trying to assure me that I was forgiven, that our bond of friendship was still intact, and that life would go on for both of us.

What a brave heart she was! What a kind and generous personality. I love her still, years later, and am still touched by her gesture toward me. After all, she had suffered great loss, and I had failed in my service to her. Yet, here she was, offering me grace.

Grace is that extension of favor and mercy, the assurance that we are loved and accepted without blame, in spite of our error. There are not words to describe how sweet it feels to know that "all is well" between us and another, even though we clearly realize that it could justly be quite different......even when the "other" is a beloved sheep.

Chapter 11: <u>Triumph!</u>

I have shared with you some of the hard things which my sheep and I encountered, but I must say, it is always those other, happier occasions which shine most brightly in my memory, and which make me smile. During the years I was a shepherd, wonderful triumphs did occur.

Once, for example, I had a newborn lamb, whom I must assume was accidentally stepped on by her mother right after delivery. When I arrived on the scene, I found a beautiful little ewe lamb with the lower half of her front leg dangling. The bone had been snapped neatly in two. It was a pitiful sight.

The lamb did not appear to be in pain, but that does not mean she was not. Remember, sheep do not cry out when they are hurting.

I felt great pity for this little lamb. I tried hard to think of what I could do help her. Rummaging around in the house I found popsicle sticks in a box of craft supplies. "Hm…," I thought. "These might work."

Back in the barn I set the lamb's front leg in the proper position. There was no wiggling on her part as I worked, and no sound came from her at all, though it must have hurt her terribly to have her leg pulled and set.

I lined up a popsicle stick on each side of her leg. I wound adhesive tape around and around it in order to keep the sticks in place.

After I had set and splinted this leg, there was nothing more to do but wait. For a couple of days the lamb got around slowly on just three legs.

Then she began, rather gingerly, to put some weight on her broken leg. By the end of a week I was amazed to see her running around with the other lambs, as though nothing bad had ever happened to her at all.

I waited a few days longer and then removed the splints. Now my little darling was just like all the other lambs, hail and hardy, and full of fun. From that time on she was perfectly normal. Even when she was an old ewe, no one could tell that her leg had ever been broken. I still feel good to think about this story with a happy ending.

Lambs usually weigh between six and nine pounds at birth. That is also just about how much human babies weigh when they are born. Of course it takes a human child about a year to be able to walk, but a lamb will most often be up and nursing within a half an hour of being born.

Low birth weight is not a good sign in either a baby or a lamb. Birth weight can be an indicator of whether or not a lamb is likely to survive or thrive. That is why, when my ewe, "Trust", delivered her first lamb, I was a bit concerned to note that the tiny creature weighed only four pounds. He looked rather like a little collector's figurine you might find on a knick knack shelf. I wondered how he could possibly make it, being so small.

I need not have worried about him, though. He was soon up and nursing. Then he was off exploring the world around him. In a short while he was bouncing along, racing up and down the barn aisles with the other lambs.

He looked rather funny because he was so small, yet he seemed singularly unaffected by his size. I named him, Mighty Mouse, even though I had promised myself never again to name any ram lamb I didn't intend to keep.

By the end of the summer, Mighty Mouse had grown a lot and was quickly closing the gap in size between himself and the other lambs. His mother was a great mom, with lots of milk and good mothering skills. "Mighty Mouse" was tiny to start with, but he more than made up for his small size by his high spirit. I can still close my eyes and picture that little bundle of energy.

Some of the most satisfying experiences I had in raising sheep were those several occasions when one sheep was willing to adopt, as her own, the lamb of another sheep. This "adoption" can be very helpful if a mother ewe is unable for some reason to nurse her lambs, or if she has had more lambs than she can reasonably care for.

Adoption does not take place naturally, however. While it may seem simple in principle, in actual practice, adoption is almost impossible to broker. The shepherd has to interfere in a serious fashion to try to accomplish it. Rarely do we succeed.

This is because each ewe knows her own lamb by its smell. The mother's bond to her own lamb is very strong and very exclusive. That means she will take good care of her own lamb, but not of any others.

Once in a while I've seen some very bold and foolish lambs attempt to nurse from a ewe who was not his or her own mother. On those occasions the ewe usually turned her head back toward the nursing lamb, put her nose close to the lamb's tail, and smelled that this was NOT her lamb. Then she delivered a head butt which rolled the intruder lamb "end over end", landing it a distance of several feet away. Ewes definitely do not like imposters when it comes to nursing lambs.

That is why convincing a ewe to accept a lamb which is not her own is difficult to do. The odds are best if the lamb which needs to be adopted is still a newborn, and if the ewe we are trying to convince to adopt has only recently lost a lamb of her own. Smearing some fluids from her dead lamb on to the new lamb can be a helpful trick, and sometimes makes a ewe think that the new lamb is also hers. It doesn't always work though.

Trust, who was little Mighty Mouse's mom, adopted a lamb for me one year.

The story started out with a terrible tragedy.

When I returned home one evening after attending my daughter's school play performance, I found that Trust had already delivered a lamb in my absence. Unfortunately, that lamb had not survived.

Seeing how upset Trust was over her loss, I hoped that another ewe would soon deliver, so I could try to give one of her lambs to Trust to raise. Sure enough, twins were born later that night.

I took one of the new twins and gave it to Trust. To my joy and surprise, she immediately accepted the newborn, without any difficulty at all. She cared for it faithfully, and raised it as her own. The lamb grew into a fine adult ewe.

I think Trust was not fooled at all by my smearing fluids from her dead lamb on to the living lamb. I think she was just a very generous personality, and was happy to have a lamb to care for.

The third year I kept sheep I bought some additional older ewes from Mr. McCoy, the farmer who had sold me my first thirteen sheep. Perhaps because there were other sheep already at our farm, these sheep seemed to adjust quickly to their new home.

I was very pleased with the new sheep, that is, until lambing began. That's when I discovered that several of these new ewes had an infection called "mastitis" in their udders.

Mastitis is a condition where the ewe's milk bag, or udder, becomes hot, lumpy and red. The tubes which deliver the milk get clogged, so that even though a sheep may have lots of milk, it cannot pass through her teats. Mastitis is very painful for the ewe, especially when her lamb tries to nurse.

Many of my ewes with mastitis would not let their lambs nurse at all. Some were able to nurse at least one lamb, if only one of her two teats was clogged, but if she had two lambs, that still meant I had to find a solution for her other lamb.

I soon became like a salesman that year, going from ewe to ewe, trying to convince my healthy ewes to adopt an extra lamb from a mastitis infected ewe. Rarely were the ewes willing to cooperate, but I kept trying, and occasionally I was successful.

In the end, I raised some of these lambs on a bottle. We called them our Bottle Babies. The problem was that there was only so much room in our old kitchen for Bottle Baby lamb pens. It became rather crowded and busy in the house.

Bottle Babies usually do not thrive as well as lambs who are raised by a ewe, so it was not a good plan to have a lot of Bottle Babies. I tried hard to place as many little ones with adoptive mothers as was possible.

One day a ewe named Annie, who had been a Bottle Baby herself a couple of years before, lost her lamb in zero degree weather. After I discovered her loss, I approached her to see if she would be willing to take a newborn whose mother had mastitis.

I rubbed fluids from Annie's dead lamb on the new lamb, and set it down by Annie's udder. Annie looked up at me as if to say, "What is that? Do you think I'm stupid or something?"

She sniffed the imposter lamb and then pushed it away with her nose. She wasn't being mean, but she also wasn't buying the proposition that she should raise this alien lamb.

Annie had a lot of milk. I knew that if she didn't take this lamb, I would have to milk her by hand so that she didn't also get mastitis.

I tried again. This time, as the lamb tried to nurse, Annie just lifted her back legs, one at a time, and stepped over the lamb and moved away from him.

She repeated this little dance several times. I was getting a bit more tired and frustrated after every attempt to convince her to accept the new lamb.

What happened next is exactly the truth, although I realize it may sound as if I am making up a story. I am not.

I sat down on the barn floor in front of Annie. "Listen, Annie!" I said. "I need your help here."

Then I explained to Annie that I was very sorry about her lost lamb. I told her that I was sorry I had not found her lamb in time to take it into the house to warm it, and possibly save it. I told her that the flock needed her help now, because some of the ewes had mastitis and could not take care of their own lambs, even though they wanted to.

Annie looked right at me and listened. I was down at her level, looking straight into her eyes.

Then I delivered what must have been the death knell to her resistance. "Just remember, Annie," I said. "When you were a lamb, you also needed help. I took you into my house. Drac tended to you, and I fed you with a bottle. Don't you think you could lend a hand now that it's your turn to help?"

I waited a moment for these words to sink in. Then I got up and positioned the newborn lamb for another try at nursing.

To my astonishment, this time Annie stood still. The lamb took hold and began to nuzzle. Soon he was drinking happily.

Annie turned her head to watch. I could see that she still wasn't thrilled over this new arrangement, but she did not side step. When her nose came close to smell the lamb, she did not butt him out of the way. Then she turned her head forward and waited.

"Thank you, Annie." I said quietly. "I know that this is hard for you, and I really appreciate it."

Chapter 12: <u>David and Buster</u>

The last ram I ever bought was a strong and handsome registered Dorset with large curled horns. I named him David because I had bought him from a farmer whose name was David. I was counting on this ram's being gentle, like the other Dorset sheep I had known. I didn't want another experience such as I had had with Arlington. I need not have worried, though. David was wonderful!

He even showed unusual interest in his offspring. He came around to visit, as it were, after each ewe delivered her lambs. He was gentle and respectful, but obviously attentive and involved. I admired him for that awareness.

As his lambs grew older, he was willing to take his turn "babysitting". One time I found him playing with a whole group of lambs, while the ewes lay resting some distance away. That really impressed me a lot.

This gathering of older lambs was not so unusual in its own right. In fact one of the absolutely most delightful things about keeping sheep was to watch the growing social activity of the lambs. They would gather together in a group, like children on a playground, while their mothers rested.

In a little while the whole group would be involved in foot races; wild, ecstatic ones, all about the barnyard. Those races began when they would all run helter skelter along an imaginary race track, and then halt abruptly at an equally imaginary finish line. Then they would turn around and, on some silent signal, race back again to where they had started.

Often they would hold their little legs stiffly, and would actually bounce, as if on springs, turning this way and that way in mid air as they moved along. It is impossible to describe adequately this charming behavior to someone who has not seen how entertaining a display of youthful lamb enthusiasm can be.

David, their sire, seemed to enjoy the antics of his lambs as much as I did. Sometimes he would join them, that is, stand in their midst as they raced around him.

I had never had a ram before who had showed the slightest interest in the lambs. Now here was David, gently touching noses with one lamb after another, even allowing them to climb over and jump off of his back as he lay on the grass. It was just delightful to see him, and I loved him all the more because of his keen attention to his "children".

One spring, a number of years after David came to our farm, my favorite and most prolific ewe, Cassi, whom you have met before, gave birth to her usual set of twins. One of the twins was a particularly handsome ram lamb. Even as a newborn, he had full shoulders and chest, sturdy legs and a straight back.

Because I had learned in my first year as a shepherd that it was hard to say "good bye" to lambs once I had named them, I rarely named a lamb unless I intended to keep it. When I dubbed this little ram lamb "Buster", just after he was born, it was because I knew right away that I was going to find a way to keep him. He was easily the finest ram lamb I had ever seen.

Cassi was a great mother sheep, and so Buster started growing very quickly. By early summer his horns began to grow, just like his father's. Soon they began to curl into large trumpets on either side of his head. It wasn't long before he began to practice butting heads with the other young rams.

A flock of sheep usually has only one, possibly two, rams at a time, so I always tried to sell the ram lambs I was not going to keep when they were around seven months old. This meant that they were gone before they grew big enough to cause trouble in the flock by fighting with the dominant ram.

Buster was not seven months old yet when he had grown to be about three fourths the size of his father. What I could not know was that long before the ram lambs were usually sold, Buster was actually going to challenge his father, David, to try to replace him as the primary ram in the flock.

It began one day when I had some visitors to the farm. We were all standing around inside the barn talking when suddenly we heard a deep resounding "THUD!" outside. The sound had been so loud that it seemed to vibrate in my bones.

I hurried outside, and then stood back in wonder as I watched Buster and David facing off a few yards away from each other, just inside the pasture fence. There they had dug in their hooves, charged directly at one another, and clashed together, head to armored head, sod flying and our ears splitting at the sound of the impact.

Then they stood frozen in dynamic tension, horn on horn, every muscle straining as each tried to shove the other off his stance. Finally they backed off, moving slowly apart without turning, and, as if on a signal from a starting gun, they charged together again. "CRASH! THUD! PUSH!"

I cannot begin to describe the energy that seemed to roll like visible shock waves in all directions; just like explosions I've seen portrayed in movies. It was very frightening, even from the relative safety of my position outside the fence. So much sheer animal power was on display.

My visitors were full of questions! I did not know what to tell them because I'd never seen anything like this before. I anticipated that young Buster was going to get his "come uppins" from his dad, as we used to say. He was, after all, still just a ram lamb, though a strapping big and strong one. He looked rather like a nervous teenaged boy who was squaring off with his father, almost as a joke.

David, on the other hand, was experienced and calm. He looked very confident and strong. I had no doubt that he could easily handle this challenge. I pictured Buster's soon being made to go back to grazing in the pasture, wiser for his brash attempts to play "king of the hill" with his father.

I knew that both rams had thick armor on their heads, and that "head on" collisions would not actually hurt either one. Usually, in cases such as this, after a few attempts one ram will tire or will sense the other's superior strength. He will signal surrender and will quit fighting. The other ram will stop charging and the battle will be over, with no one hurt.

To my amazement, however, this isn't what happened with David and Buster. Over and over again Buster charged, backed off, and then charged again.

David stayed attentive, parried the blows, but did not seem to be too concerned about the final outcome. Like the good father he was, David was giving Buster practice in the art of self defense, but he, himself, was not being overly aggressive toward his son.

Then the scene suddenly changed. Somehow or another, Buster got in one lucky freak blow to David's rear quarter. I watched as the larger ram's legs began to buckle and he nearly fell. He recovered his balance quickly, but during the next charge and the next, I could see that David had been weakened by that one lucky hit to his body.

Though I had begun watching this extraordinary display utterly convinced that David would easily win, now the tide had turned. David was now really being seriously challenged. His intensity changed and he began to try to fight vigorously. His stance had been affected, however. Now he could not charge as well, or hold his straining position as long.

Buster seemed to sense the change, and, instead of backing off, became emboldened by his unlikely success. He was now not only charging head to head, but was again attempting to catch David off guard with a body blow.

I instantly realized with alarm that Buster could actually do David great harm if he insisted on taking this battle to a new level, and if he succeeded in getting past David's weakened defenses. Buster was no longer just sparring with his "Old Man". He had begun to challenge David seriously for the position of dominate ram in the flock.

I was beginning to feel a little sick to my stomach with concern for my dear old ram. This was a dangerous and unexpected turn of events. I sensed a need to intervene quickly. I did not want David to be hurt, or possibly even killed.

I felt responsible for the bad situation, because, I was realizing too late, I should have separated the two rams earlier, and put one of them in a pen in the barn by himself. I had never dreamed a partly grown ram lamb would, or could, do the kind of damage Buster now seemed bent on doing.

I knew that I'd better do something quickly. But do what? I had no idea!

It would be insane for me to step between these two combatants who were so intent on each other that they might not even see me coming toward them. Furthermore, no force I knew of would be able to hold them back from what had now become a serious conflict. I tried to think of what to do.

I quickly realized that when David and Buster actually engaged each other, and were pushing hard, head to head, they might be very easily rolled over on to their backs, if we could grab them from the side. Once knocked off their feet, they would both be helpless.

The plan formed itself in my mind. This would not be the first time I had toppled a big ram off his feet. It would, however, definitely be the scariest time. Both rams would have to be toppled at the same time, or it could be very dangerous for everyone.

I enlisted the help of a couple of my able bodied visitors. I told them what we would have to do, and sure enough, the next time the rams engaged, literally, in head to head combat, we hurried to their sides. Next we reached under their bellies, grabbed their far hind legs and toppled them easily onto their backs.

The battle was all over in a second. Looking back, I want to believe that I did not expose my visitors to too much danger.

I was deeply relieved, to be certain, but now I had to make another decision in a hurry. Which ram should I lead from the pasture?

David had been defeated, and soundly! Young as he was, Buster had won the day.

If the battle had taken place in the wild, this would have been David's last day on the job, if not his last day, period. It had been a shocking, stunning experience for me too.

Since I had expected Buster eventually to replace David as dominant ram, I decided that "eventually" had just been moved up to "today". The timing of this move had been by Buster's choice, not mine.

As I led poor David away, my visitors continued to hold Buster on his back. They did not let him get up until David and I were through the gate and out of sight.

I put a harness on David and tied him to a tree in the front yard, where he could see neither the barn nor the pasture. Most especially, I placed him where Buster could not see him.

I have never seen a sadder animal in my life. David lay low on the ground, with his chin between his front feet. He didn't want food. He didn't want water. He looked off in the distance blankly, as if he just wanted to die. I felt so sorry for him.

I spent time with David over the next several days. I told him that I had placed an ad in the county newspaper, and that I was looking to find a new home for him. Maybe he felt that I had betrayed him, but really, I think he knew that this was just the natural way of things.

Buster, meanwhile, was playing "cock of the walk" out there in the pasture. The ewes seemed to have accepted the change in personnel, and to the unknowing eye, everything appeared normal. It was anything but normal for poor David, however.

A few days later a truck pulled up to my back door. In it was a couple from the mainland who had answered my ad in the paper. When they saw David they were just thrilled. "What a marvelous, handsome ram.! Yes, we would like to take him."

As if David understood that he was being admired and appreciated again, he promptly stood up and showed these new folks how truly magnificent he actually was. It was remarkable how quickly his mood changed. I think he was excited to be getting on with his new situation.

I told him "good bye", and that I loved him. I promised him that he would soon be happy again. Then the truck drove off and he was gone.

A few weeks later his new owners called to tell me how pleased all their ewes had been to "make David's acquaintance". They told me that he seemed to be very happy. His day of disgrace was a faint memory to him now as he took up his important position with his new flock.

Buster, meanwhile, lived up to all the expectations I ever had for a ram. He was gentle and responsive. His lambs were beautiful. He was attentive to his family, just as his father had been before him. I was proud of him too!

It turned out that Buster was actually the last ram I had. The time came that I had to sell my entire flock. When that time came, Buster went on the truck along with the ewes. His new owners were also thrilled to have him.

It occurred to me that, just as Buster had replaced David as the dominant ram of the flock, so too, the time had come when other people replaced me as the shepherd of my flock. It seems that change is always taking place. Sometimes that change is pleasant, and sometimes it is quite difficult.

After I sold my flock I missed my sheep very much, but my family's needs were a greater priority than was my "childhood dream come true." The end had come for this adventure. When my turn came to leave my leadership position with the flock, I tried to be as accepting of the change as David came to be of his.

Did I mention how much I really loved that ram?

Chapter 13: <u>My Friend, Ingrid</u>

Shepherds have been looking after sheep since ancient times. In many parts of the world shepherds still tend sheep in much the same ways they have for centuries.

Even in our country in modern times, being a shepherd is very hard work. Doing it all alone is next to impossible. Shepherds need companions to help them, especially when they face emergency situations.

I am very blessed to have had a shepherd friend on the Island who lived just up the hill and across the road from me. Her name is Ingrid, and we helped each other a lot.

When Ingrid had to go away for a few days, I looked after her flock. She did the same for me when my turn came. It was always something of an adventure for us to care for each other's sheep. Ingrid's flock tolerated me, and my flock tolerated her, but the sheep were never very happy about the "substitute shepherd" routine. They wanted their own shepherd to attend to them.

Besides, we did things differently, and we laughed a lot about that too. When Ingrid wanted her sheep to follow her, she banged on a bucket, and then fed her sheep a little grain out of that same bucket. After a while, they learned to follow the sound of the banging, even if nothing were in the bucket at all. Her sheep followed Ingrid anywhere, as long as she kept up the noise. I thought it was rather humorous to watch.

After Drac died, however, I, on the other hand, got behind my flock and made a noise, sometimes actually banging on a bucket also. My sheep moved away from me in the direction I wanted them to go, as long as I kept up the noise. Come to think of it, I'll bet Ingrid thought I was rather funny to watch in action also.

Ingrid began to keep sheep about the same time I did. As we worked together, we became the best of friends, and were each other's most dependable source of help with our sheep.

Ingrid had four young children at the time. She was both a devoted mother, and a caring and very competent shepherd. We got along together splendidly.

Asking help from one another was no small matter. After all, it meant saying to a friend, "Will you please volunteer to get hot, sweaty, dead tired and incredibly dirty for my sake, as you help me to take care of my sheep?" Assisting in an emergency could take all day, or all night, for that matter. Ingrid and I were always willing to "be there for each other", as people say.

Ingrid had Suffolk sheep, a breed with black faces and legs, whose ears tend to hang down. As I've told you before, I originally had Columbia sheep. They are a breed whose bodies are all white, and whose ears tend to stand up.

Ingrid and I each favored our own breed, of course. We sometimes joked around with each other about which breed was the better. Well, to be honest, we joked around a whole lot about almost everything. When two friends spend as much time together as we did, getting filthy dirty and tired, there just wasn't much we couldn't say to one another, and most of it was very humorous.

The best part about our helping each other was that we really knew and understood how much our sheep meant to us. We fought as hard to save sheep from the other's flock as we fought to save our own. It was very satisfying to work together.

Now, I don't mean to make too much of it, but most of the other farmers on the Island raised cattle. We'd see those farmers in town or at church, and while a number of them were very supportive of our endeavors, a couple of them would tend to ask rather curious questions about how it was going in the sheep business. We soon got the idea that maybe they were really asking, "Are you ready to give up yet?" Their hints only made us all the more determined NEVER to give up.

Once I engaged one of these cattle farmers to come put a couple loads of gravel around in my barnyard to improve drainage when it rained. It was plain that he didn't know anything about sheep, because he drove his big front end loader right into the barnyard without even letting me know he had arrived.

When my sheep saw that gigantic yellow machine approaching, they panicked. They dove right through the fences, and scattered all over the farm. Many of them were cut up in the process, and some were bleeding.

This neighbor thought the stampede was just hilarious. He sat up there on his big piece of equipment, laughing out loud.

I was NOT laughing! I wanted to yell at him, and to tell him how mean I thought he was. Instead, because I sensed that his actions may have been meant to tease me, I just bit my tongue and tried not to let him know what I was really feeling. He was doing me a favor, I allowed, and I at least needed to be grateful for that.

He finally finished his work and left. It took me most of the remainder of the day to round up my frightened sheep and get them back together in the barnyard. None of them was seriously injured, but they remained very skittish for days afterward.

Ingrid was as angry as I was, after she heard my story. We decided we would try to do everything we could by ourselves, and would not ask for help any more from our neighbors, unless it were absolutely necessary.

One night, early in our shepherding careers, I called Ingrid because I had a ewe in labor, and things didn't appear to be going well. At that time neither of us was yet a very experienced lamb midwife. I wanted Ingrid's opinion on what might be wrong with my ewe, and what I could do about it.

It was winter, and so we arrived at my barn dressed in snow pants, hats, gloves, boots, sweaters and coats. A couple of hours later, having shed all those outer garments one by one, we managed to pull three lambs from an exhausted ewe.

We looked at each other and started to laugh. Everything we still wore was wet and smelly. So were we! We were headed for the showers, but three healthy lambs were already on their feet beside us. We grinned at each other in glee.

On another occasion our similar efforts ended in tragedy. That time one of my ewes had also delivered triplets. The lambs were already up and nursing when Drac came around the corner, as he often did, to have a look. Never before, and never again, but on this particular occasion, this particular ewe went into a full fledged panic. She began running furiously around her birthing pen in tight circles, and then she collapsed and died right at my feet.

Our frantic efforts, first to stop her, then to revive her, failed. Ingrid and I were wet and filthy, as usual, but this time there was no grin of triumph. I was in anguish over what we had just witnessed, but could not prevent.

Three healthy, but now orphaned, lambs stood beside us calling softly for their mamma. It was terrible.

After a few years there were some other Islanders who became interested in raising sheep. Our friend, Bill, had a small flock of exotic Icelandic sheep, so famous for their wool. The fourth flock on the Island was owned by Lee and Karin, who also kept some cattle.

One friend became a goatherd. Susan, a lovely writer who had moved to the Island from New Mexico, was put in charge of quite a large herd of Angora goats, a business venture of her brother's. We thought that she was especially brave, knowing what we knew about goats.

Ingrid and I, as the "old timers", taught these new shepherds what we knew, and helped out our friends whenever we could. It was fun now for Ingrid and me to have a little group of fellow shepherds to share our stories and equipment with from time to time.

Upon reflection, I realize that it wasn't just Ingrid's help that meant so much to me. It was that we were sharing together in something we both loved very much. That companionship and sharing made the good experiences twice as good, and the bad experiences half as bad as they otherwise would have been. It seems almost miraculous how that worked out.

Ingrid had her share of disasters too. One time she bought some new ewes, and only later found that they were all infected with a disease. She needed to separate them from her original flock, so she rented a pasture from a neighbor who wasn't farming. I helped her to build the fences, and then helped her to fight for the lives of her sheep.

She lost a number of them anyway. I understood how bad she felt about it.

Ingrid learned to spin her own yarn from the wool of her sheep. I bought a knitting machine and began making hats and sweaters from yarn I had paid to have spun commercially from my wool.

My yarn was all white, and Ingrid had some naturally colored yarn. We traded yarn back and forth.

Ingrid dreamed up an idea, and then together we made and sold quite a number of comforters. They were filled with fluffy wool batting and covered with soft cotton flannel.

I gave Ingrid's children piano lessons. She kept me supplied with produce from her garden, wondrous baked goods from her kitchen, and great books from her amazing library.

One day Ingrid called me on the phone. She sounded upset. "My husband has a new job," she cried. "We're moving to town!"

"Oh, no!" I pleaded. "I don't want you to leave the Island."

The sheep! She couldn't move the sheep to town. She would have to give up the sheep. I would have to give up Ingrid. I didn't even want to think about it.

Of course Ingrid and her family did move to town. A few years later I also had to give up my flock.

I remember the day the truck come to take my whole flock away to their new owner. I jumped into the shower just as they drove down the lane. I didn't want anybody to see how hard I was crying.

The amazing adventure I had begun so many years before was now over. I grieved for many days. It was very hard to let go of all my wooly friends. I missed them a lot.

There is a season to most things, however, and gradually I realized that the season of my being a shepherd was over. How thankful I felt that my childhood dream had indeed come true. I had been a shepherd, just as I had planned when I was five years old. That dream's being fulfilled was something to treasure and to celebrate.

Ingrid and I are still great friends. We don't see each other as often as we once did, but we still laugh and giggle when we get together.

Her children are all grown up now. They are wonderful adults. I always knew they would be.

Ingrid now works as an advocate for disabled people. She looks after their needs, and helps them to get the services they are entitled to receive.

I am a school teacher again. I also do volunteer work, advocating for disadvantaged adults and children.

One day Ingrid and I realized that we are still "shepherds", in a manner of speaking. We may have changed the make up of our flocks, but not the make up of our work. We still tend to the needs of others. Sometimes we have triumphs, and sometimes we have tragedies. We continue to support each other.

Being a shepherd of sheep is very hard work, and, as you have seen, it is often disappointing and sad. The same can be said of working with people. Sometimes we still get discouraged, and often we get very tired.

Ingrid and I know that the lessons we learned while caring for sheep help us to care well for people. We know that we still need to do all we can to help our "flock", but that sometimes our best will not be enough to bring us total success. We have learned to accept that truth, and when it happens, to pick up and continue our work, giving thanks for each new opportunity.

And yet there are wonderful times too, times when things do go right, and when people are helped or, better yet, learn to help themselves. When that occurs, Ingrid and I still have occasion to grin in glee.

Who would have thought that my dream of being a shepherd would have turned out this way? I never did......, but I'm very respectful when I hear a child tell me that he or she has a dream of doing something "when I grow up". I always encourage that child to hold on to the dream. I did, and I am very thankful for the results that arose from a "childhood dream come true."

Chapter 14: <u>Maize and Miss Marvel</u>

Here is my story.
I know that it's true,
for I saw it happen,
so I'll tell it to you.

Most sheep have their lambs
in winter or spring.
A lamb in the summer's a
a marvelous thing!

So that's what we named her.
(She came in late June.)
We called her "Miss Marvel."
She proved her name soon,

for out in the pasture,
with all of the flock,
the cattle, our pony,
Miss Marvel now walked,

so sweet and so dainty,
so helpless and frail,
with little wool coat
and tiny bobbed tail.

We stood by the fence
and we watched her go by,
then gazed at some vultures
way up in the sky.

And what happened next
folks will never believe,
but I tell the truth,
I won't ever deceive.

The vultures flew down
and attacked our dear lamb.
My son called to me,
"Run as fast as you can!"

But before I could reach her,
a stunning surprise,
our old pony, "Maize",
with fire in her eyes

came thundering forward
with trumpeting call.
She snorted her warning
with every hoof fall,

and wheeling and rearing
she entered the fray.
As quick as a wink
those big birds flew away.

Poor Marvel was bleeding
and bleating some too.
We needed to help her,
but what could we do,

for Maize was so angry
she couldn't see straight.
She kept charging & pawing,
then she'd whinny and wait.

My son and his friends
tried to pick up the lamb,
but Maize chased them out
of the pasture again.

So I talked to her gently
and gave her my thanks.
She'd rescued Miss Marvel
and I think she ranks

with the animal heroes
of ancient wild yarns.
I told her so, softly, as
we walked toward the barn.

Miss Marvel is grown now.
Do you think she looks back
on her close brush with death
and a pony's brave act?

I'm not sure she does,
but I know I still do,
and now you know the story
for I've told it to you.

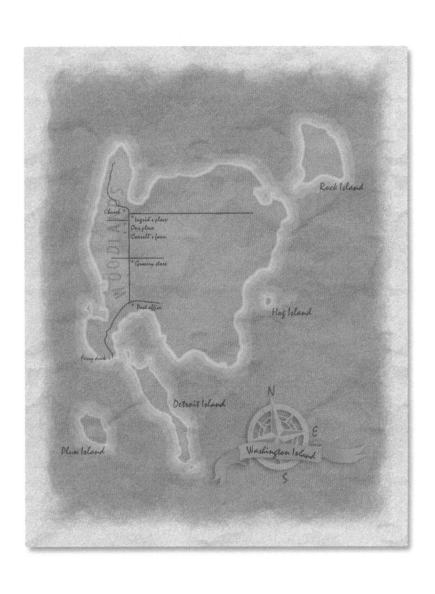

Glossary

1. amniotic fluid - the watery fluid which surrounds an unborn lamb

2. aurora - the aurora borealis, sometimes called the Northern Lights

3. bale - a tied up package of hay (or other materials)

4. biography - the written account of a person's life

5. biology - the science of life and life processes

6. bladder - a membrane sac which holds a sheep's urine before voiding

7. bloat - to swell up with liquid or gas, causing great pain or even death

8. body language - posture betraying how an animal (or person) is feeling

9. breed - domestic animals with similarly inherited characteristics

10. browsing - to feed on leaves, twigs and shoots of shrubs or bushes

11. carriers - one who has the gene for a deformity, but not exhibiting it

12. colostrum - the first milk secreted by a ewe after giving birth to a lamb

13. Columbia sheep - large, white American breed, gentle and fast growing

14. comforters - warm blanket made with covering and interior loose wool

15. contractions - squeezing of abdominal muscles to expel lamb at birth

16. corn starch - white powder made from starchy part of corn kernel

17. dam - mother sheep

18. deformed - twisted or bent bones in a sheep

19. delivery - the passage of the lamb from inside mother sheep in birthing

20. docking - cutting or pinching tail from lamb

21. dominate ram - the strongest ram in a flock

22. Dorset sheep - a large English breed of sheep known for good mothering

23. elimination - excreting waste products, urine or feces, from the body

24. escapade - a carefree or reckless adventure

25. ewe - a female sheep

26. fallow - land which has been tilled but not seeded with a crop

27. feigning - to give a false impression, to pretend

28. fiber arts - the crafts related to fibers, ex.: spinning, weaving, knitting

29. flabbergasted - to be absolutely astonished

30. fleece - the coat of wool of a sheep or similar animal

31. flock - a group of sheep that live, travel and feed together

32. fly strike - an attack of egg laying flies on an animal's skin

33. front end loader - earth moving equipment with front, movable bucket

34. gene - an heredity unit which determines animal characteristics

35. genetics - study of how an organism's development is affected by genes

36. glaciers - a huge mass of moving ice formed from compacted snow

37. gluttony - eating or drinking too much

38. gorge - eating or drinking too much on one occasion

39. granary - a building for storing grain

40. grazing - to feed on growing grasses and low growing plants

41. Hampshire sheep - a large English meat breed known for fast growth

42. haunches - the hip, buttock and upper thigh of a animal (or person)

43. hay - grasses or other plants which are cut and dried for animal food

44. herd - a group of cattle or goats which live, travel and feed together

45. infestation - to be overrun with large numbers of pests, such as flies

46. injection - forcing medicine with a needle into a muscle or under skin

47. intestinal - having to do with an animal's (or a human's) intestines

48. instincts - the untrained impulses which influence animal behavior

49. kidneys - the organs which regulate body water and acid/base balance

50. knick knack - a small ornamental trinket

51. labor - the period during which a sheep's body births a lamb

52. lamb - a baby sheep

53. leached - to be dissolved and washed out by a liquid passing through

54. legume - plants of the botanical family which includes peas and clover

55. manure - animal excreted wastes

56. mastitis - inflammation of a sheep's udder

57. Mensa - international group whose members must have a high IQ

58. Merino sheep - a Spanish breed known for its excellent wool

59. mold - any of a variety of funguses which destroy organic matter

60. mucus - protective lubricating coating secreted by mucous membrane

61. pasture - land dedicated to growing plants meant for grazing animals

62. poison ivy - American shrub or vine which can cause a rash on contact

63. predators - animals which live by preying on other animals, ex. coyote

64. profitable - capable of producing a profit, of earning money or benefit

65. ram - a male sheep

66. registered - being recognized and listed with a breeders' organization

67. resuscitation - to restore consciousness to an animal (or human)

68. Saanen goat - a Swiss breed of dairy goats; short white hair, no horns

69. sacrifice - giving up a thing of great value to gain one of greater value

70. salvation - rescuing something or someone from danger or destruction

71. selenium - a nonmetallic element needed by animals in small amounts

72. sentry - a guard posted to keep watch against intruders

73. shears - modern electrified scissors used to cut wool from a sheep

74. sheepish - becoming embarrassed over realizing a mistake or fault

75. shepherd - one who herds, cares for and guards sheep

76. siesta - a rest, usually taken after the midday meal

77. sire - father

78. sparse - growing at wide spaced intervals

79. spasm - an uncontrollable, involuntary muscle contraction

80. straw - the stem of a cereal grain, used for bedding animals

81. suffocate - to die from lack of air

82. Sulfolk sheep - a popular English breed of meat sheep with black faces

83. temperament - the characteristic behavior of a sheep (or a human)

84. toxins - a dangerous poisonous substance secreted by certain organisms

85. umbilical cord - an unborn lamb's lifeline to its mother's body

86. uterus - the organ which holds an unborn lamb while it is developing

87. vet - abbreviation for veterinarian, or animal physician

88. White Muscle disease - a fatal condition caused by a lack of selenium

89. yarn - thread spun from wool fibers, used for weaving and knitting

Made in the USA
Charleston, SC
17 September 2015